The Self-Confident Woman

The Self-Confident Woman

Janet Congo, M.A.

Life Journey™

Life Journey is an imprint of
Cook Communications Ministries, Colorado Springs, Colorado 80918
Cook Communications, Paris, Ontario
Kingsway Communications, Eastbourne, England

THE SELF-CONFIDENT WOMAN

First Printing, 2003
Printed in the United States of America

1 2 3 4 5 6 7 8 9 10 Printing/Year 07 06 05 04 03

Senior Editor: Janet Lee
Editor: Susan H. Miller
Cover & Interior Design: Andrea L. Boven, Boven Design Studio, Inc.

Library of Congress Cataloging-in-Publication Data

Congo, Janet, 1949-
The self-confident woman / Janet Congo.
p. cm.
Includes bibliographical references.
ISBN 0-7814-3869-1 (pbk.)
1. Christian women—Religious life. 2. Self-perception in women—Religious aspects—Christianity. I. Title.
BV4527.C6438 2003
248.8'43—dc21

2003006450

CONTENTS

DEDICATION

To AMY
My precious daughter,
a woman of faith, intelligence,
creativity, beauty and courage.
A new bride.
Always remember that you are loved!

ACKNOWLEDGMENTS

It is with deep gratitude and appreciation that I acknowledge the contributions of the following people to this manuscript:

To Dave Congo for his extensive theological and psychological counsel; Janet Lee, a gifted editor for her sensitive and professional assistance; and H. Norman Wright, for his willingness to review the manuscript.

To the numerous women who willingly attended seminars based on this content—I'm grateful for your questions, comments and prayers.

To my parents and Dave's parents for their loving support and affirmation; Jean Coffin, for being a thoughtful critic and a cherished friend; and Bonnie Prietto, for her timely help in data entry and formatting on the computer.

FOREWORD

by H. Norman Wright

Jan has a unique and insightful ability to put her finger on the unique concerns and struggles of women. Not only that, she isn't hesitant to address issues that so many woman have wanted to hear discussed in a healthy manner for years.

This book doesn't center on theory but practicality. It puts the reader into action by the way the chapters are constructed. Then it has potential to give the reader a way to change their life. Chapters are brief which will enable anyone to retain what was read.

Many books today claim to have a biblical basis but often just tuck in a verse here and there. Not this one! Jan has made sure that what she says is thoroughly grounded in Scripture and encourages the reader to center her life in Christ.

Anyone reading this book will be challenged to think and reflect but will also be thankful for its existence.

INTRODUCTION

Different women, different voices:

- "I'm so stupid. How could I have been dumb enough to say that?"
- "How come he left me for her? What am I, chopped liver?"
- "I don't know who I am anymore."
- "I've lost me. My kids are off to college. I barely know my husband."
- "Am I all washed up? How can I love him and not lose me? Is it even possible?"
- "I'm always the third wheel. When am I going to find a man?"
- "I've always been married and now Tom is gone. Who am I? Where do I fit?"

Does any of this sound familiar? If so, my heart goes out to you. There is little more painful than feeling as if you have disappeared or that the "you" who exists is a total and complete screw-up. It hurts to be asked the simple question, "How are you?" You want to run and hide because the questioner might see the despair in your eyes. After all, you're a Christian. How in the world could things have gotten to this place?

It hurts to wake up some mornings. You've lost the excitement of being you. Your three year old says his prayers one night and his words, "Thank you, God, that I like me!" prompt you to flee the room before he can ask what's wrong. You're sobbing from the depths of your being.

If you have picked up this book, there is a reason—a good reason. You want to be a confident woman: confident in God's love, confident in your own abilities and gifts, confident in your place in your significant relationships and in your world. I applaud you. I want that for you too, and I believe from the depths of my heart that God wants that for you.

Don't assume that because I am writing this book I've never struggled with my self-esteem and my place in the world. Just the opposite is true, as you will discover from reading these pages. What I have come to see personally is that almost everything in our world works against us on this score. Parents, brothers and sisters, girlfriends, boyfriends, employers, relatives, spouses and ex-spouses, children, and even some in the church attempt in subtle and not-so-subtle ways to let us know that we don't quite measure up. Some go so far as to attempt to mold us into their images. How does this happen? It's simple. Everyone on planet Earth is dealing with the same issues. All humans at various points in time question their worth and value. Research suggests that 95% of Americans struggle with feelings of inadequacy and the other 5% are liars. We are all imperfect, incomplete, immature, and—dare I say it—insecure.

This book is designed to counteract these voices and help you find your own voice. It is meant to be read and studied, worked out in your journal and lived out in your life. My journey has taught me the truth of the seeming contradiction found in the book of Philippians: "Therefore, my dear friends, as you have always obeyed—not only in my presence, but now much more in my absence—continue to *work out your salvation* with fear and trembling, *for it is God who works in you* to will and to act according to his good purpose" (Philippians 2:12–13, emphasis mine).

When I first read these verses, I wanted to question the Apostle Paul. Whose work is it anyway, Paul? Is it God's or is it mine? Over my lifetime, I have come to see with Paul that it is both. God has committed to work in me, but I also have a part in the process.

This book has three major sections. Section 1, "Distortions," examines how easy it is to be confused about our identity and who we are in relationships. Everywhere we turn, someone else has an opinion. As if that isn't enough to keep us off balance, we live in a culture that perpetuates the lie that we must earn our value. The voices of the people who "know" turn our heads with their perspectives about how we should look or act, or what we should own and do. All this fuels our insecurity.

Section 2, "Reality," deals with the truth that God, in the person of Jesus Christ, must be the foundation on which I build my identity. Whatever (or whomever) is the center of my life determines how I define myself, and the value I ascribe to myself. Jesus is the only one whose control will make me more of what I was created to be. His control empowers me rather than destroys me.

As central as I believe this truth is to who I am as a woman, it is not enough to nod my head in intellectual agreement. My belief must be backed up by my actions in the trenches of life and in the context of relationships. For this reason, in the third section of this book, "Reality Becomes Action," I offer myself as a coach assisting you in taking 30 steps necessary to bring the reality of action to the reality of belief in the area of your self-concept. As I cheer you on, as you are personally faithful with the journaling exercises provided, and as you are supported by women on a similar journey, God will work in you in ways that you can now only imagine.

I invite you to embark upon a day-by-day, moment-by-moment journey towards confidence. I will be honored if you will allow me to be your personal coach.

Because God transforms,
Janet M. Congo

WHAT YOU WILL NEED TO BEGIN

- A blank journal
- A pad of lined paper
- Pencils, pens, and an eraser
- Sticky Notes
- A supportive friend or family member to be your prayer partner
- If possible, a small group with whom you can embark upon this training program

Part One

DISTORTIONS

DISTORTIONS: CONFUSING MESSAGES

What happens when you bend over a baby girl's bassinet and begin talking to her? It's as if you bring life out of her. Her eyes sparkle, every part of her body registers excitement, and the most beautiful smile spreads across her little face. Both of you feel more alive. Both of you benefit from this enchanting moment.

God made us for relationship with Him and each other. In the creation story, God presents Eve to Adam because, "It is not good for man to be alone" (Genesis 2:18). Relationships teach us whether the world is a safe place, where we fit in, and who we are in that world.

CONTRADICTIONS CREATE CONFUSION

Being a child can be very difficult and oh, so confusing. Not one of us has had or is a perfect parent. Adult behavior is inconsistent, frightening, perplexing, and inexplicable. The same parents who talk about loving us forever decide they don't love each other. Divorce shatters a child's world.

A child may have an emotionally detached parent. No matter what she does, the parent withholds approval. She feels invisible and unimportant. Some little girls face the agony of watching a parent die. Reality renders them helpless.

So many things don't make sense. A little girl may find herself being negatively compared to a sibling or another child. She can't understand why. She only knows that she doesn't measure up. Parental neglect, rejection, or sexual, physical, or emotional abuse all leave the child doubting herself. Because she is still dependent on the parent, she makes the parent "good" and herself "bad."

Mother may stress the value of honesty. Yet innocently the little one walks into a room and overhears her mom talking on the phone. Mother tells her friend something that the child knows isn't true. She searches her mom's face, waiting for an explanation. None is forthcoming. The hypocrisy isn't even acknowledged.

This same precious little girl goes to school. She adores her teacher. One day the teacher is sarcastic and belittles the child, who shrinks in shame. The child dares to ask, "Don't you like me?" Instead of apologizing for her remarks, the teacher spouts a platitude about liking all of her students. The little girl knows differently. Yet this is the teacher who stresses "using your voices respectfully and kindly." How does the little girl put it all together?

Then her best friend becomes friends with another little girl who doesn't like her. Her friend calls her horrible names and starts to spread rumors about her. She is devastated. Her heart is broken. She runs home that day in need of reassurance and for some reason her mom isn't there.

What does the little girl do with the inconsistencies, the contradictions, and the hypocrisy? Questions bombard her mind. How do I fit in? Who can I trust? Is safety possible? Am I loved? Am I important? How do I make sense of it all?

Children who face so many inconsistencies that they can't make sense of them often deny reality and sacrifice their will to understand. They stop questioning reality. They just attempt to fit in. The rest of us, who face only a few inconsistencies, are left confused and at times overwhelmed. Our awareness and our self-esteem suffer.

CULTURAL MESSAGES CREATE CONFUSION

The little girl who loves to hang upside down from trees, play in the mud, and entertain her stuffed animals also exists in a cultural context. Her church, along with her culture, seems to value "niceness," compliance and passivity in little girls. Her pastor talks about how valuable we all are to God, but it seems that mostly men go into ministry. She wonders if men really are more important to God.

When she encounters conflict, she learns that it is "unladylike" to fight back. It isn't okay to say "No," especially to adults. Often she learns that the "world" is something she can't trust, while she should trust the "church." Yet she sees people hurt others even in the church.

Even her pastor describes women as emotional and overly sensitive while men are logical and rational. Those words feel like an insult to her, but she isn't sure why. She listens as guys demean and devalue females. Sometimes it's even fathers and brothers who call girls bad names and talk about abusing them.

Fairy tales leave her dreaming of a Prince Charming who will sweep into her life, tell her she's the "fairest in the land," and make her life perfect. Over the radio waves she hears words like, "I can't live if living is without you!" Her friends flock to Britney Spear's concerts and hear her sing, "I'm your slave" while swaying her "perfect," scantily dressed body. Repeatedly the themes of movies and novels have to do with a woman surrendering who she is or what she values in order to get love. Highly publicized romances between celebrity couples often emphasize choosing style over substance.

Our churches hold up marriage as the highest of all relationships. Yet as the little girl sits in church, many of the messages on marriage are similar. The theme seems to be "women, submit." Submission seems to mean "giving in and giving up." Somehow the little girl picks up a sense that if she doesn't have a man or if she isn't in a relationship she is flawed and incomplete. So the little girl dreams while playing wedding on the floor with her Barbie dolls of someday being swept off her feet by a wonderful guy.

ADOLESCENCE CREATES CONFUSION

During the adolescent years young women begin to look to interpersonal relationships rather than achievements for a sense of self. Relationships, especially with guys, begin to take on great importance. It's not unusual to see a girl collapse emotionally if her relationship fails.

By the time girls reach junior high, and especially in high school, they seem to have their antennas up searching for male approval. They put on makeup, worry about weight, wear uncomfortable, suggestive clothes and choose shoes that make their feet scream. Why? In order to get noticed. A compliment or a put down from a guy carries far more weight than the same thing from a girl.

Much of society, including the church, values "nice" over "honest." Since they must not hurt anyone's feelings, girls learn to be indirect and to tell "white" lies. To be different, confrontational, or too strong is frowned upon. In fact, young women must not appear "too" anything—too courageous, too outspoken, too enthusiastic, too emotional or too smart. Adolescent girls try to imitate other girls they admire. They must not stick out, but they must be noticed.

Ever so subtly, the young woman distances herself from her ideas and from her voice in order to gain approval and be worthy of male attention. She tries to be someone she isn't. Her self-esteem suffers. Being accepted and loved is essential for feeling good about herself, and even then there is always something that she would like to change about herself.

Reminiscing about the confusion of adolescence led one woman to write these words:

> When I was a little girl, I had lofty ambitions. I wanted to lead armies, to vanquish the bad guys, and be not the fairest, but the bravest in the land. But something happened on my way to teenagehood. My spirit shrank to the size of a thimble. I became preoccupied with how I looked, with fitting in and being popular, especially with boys. I kept my deepest thoughts and feelings to myself, because they no longer seemed suitable. After awhile I didn't really know what I thought or felt. My inner voice grew silent.
>
> JANE FONDA[1]

When a young woman is separated from her voice she loses connection with herself and with others. She leaves the power of self–definition and self-control at the door and hands that power to others. After all, nothing is more important than being chosen and belonging.

On an "Oprah" show on female teens abused by their boyfriends, a sickening statistic suggested that one in four teenage girls is a victim of dating violence before they leave high school. Perhaps some girls will put up with even the most brutal behavior rather than to be without a boyfriend.

Amazing pressure can even come from the women in a young woman's life. When my daughter was enjoying a fabulous friendship with her first boyfriend, another woman asked me if I thought this would be her first sexual experience. A friend of my daughter received a gift for high school graduation—a "boob job"—breast implants. The donor was none other than the young woman's grandmother. Strong messages come from older women to our daughters.

YOUNG ADULTHOOD CREATES CONFUSION

These same young women leave home to go off to college or into their first apartments and their first jobs. They are both excited and terrified. They always are on the lookout for "The One." In the process, they attempt to attract and please. They are on constant diets; they drop previously make plans to spend time with a guy; they often feel as if they have to compete with other women, and they treat their women friends as if they are expendable if the guy becomes available.

Many young women have a tendency to become involved with men too quickly and too intensely. Even the young women who have multiple interests seem to spend most of their time talking about their current love, the one who just left them, or the one they want to have.

In the counseling office I often ask clients in a long-term relationship if and when they became sexually involved. It's not unusual to hear a pause and then, "We waited a long time." When I ask, "How long?" the answer is often, "a month." Once sex enters the dating relationship it becomes central. All other ways of knowing each other—intellectual, spiritual and emotional—take a back seat.

Many Christian young women who have ignored their own value system, lowered their defenses, and become sexually involved prior to marriage are devastated with guilt. They blame themselves, become depressed, and their self-esteem plummets. This causes them to become more dependent and less willing to risk rejection and abandonment. At that point they often try to make the young man fit their fantasy rather than seeing clearly who he is and that he also didn't stick to his value system.

When their friends become engaged, young women often feel an amazing pressure to find a romantic attachment quickly. They try to get power, talent, accomplishments, and wealth from this person. Others let themselves be bought with expensive dinners, vacations, and gifts. Many let the man in their life make decisions for them and thereby establish a precedent for the rest of their relationship.

Young women who do not have a "significant other" often feel "less than" those who do. By the time these gals are in their early thirties panic fills them.

Women crave relationship. Relationship can either call us to life, to help us be more of who we truly are, or relationships can zap the life from us. It all depends on whether we disappear or whether we show up.

In order to have a sense of the person we are uniquely created to be, we must first learn who we are separate from others. Mark Twain said, "The worst loneliness is not to be comfortable with yourself." Therein lies a problem. Many of us have spent our youths searching for that special person with whom we will spend the rest of our lives. We spend far less energy discovering who it is that we are. What that means is that often marriage is the place where we finally learn who we are, separate from that man we love. Rarely, if ever, do we anticipate when we say "I do" that we have that kind of learning ahead of us.

TEACHING CREATES CONFUSION

We attended a wedding where the pastor addressed the bride and groom with these words, "You are to be involved in a partnership marriage." Turning to the young man he said, "You will be the head partner." Next he addressed the bride, "And you, my dear, will be the silent partner."

Our own pre-marital counseling set us on an unhealthy path. Both of us were committed Christians, we really loved each other and we wanted to make our marriage a great one according to God's standards. The pastor told Dave that if ours was to be a Christian marriage, he was to serve God. I, on the other hand, was instructed to serve Dave. Today we see that as a twisted interpretation of Scripture. At that time, however, we swallowed this teaching hook, line, and sinker.

Any woman subjected to this teaching comes to believe that she has only one option. Believing this view of submission leads to an unhealthy dependence. The woman must surrender and submit all to this young man she must spend her life serving. Other women find the thought of such a chameleon like stance appalling and decide that their only option is to go to the other extreme and to be independent, because they're certainly not going to be dependent.

The dependent woman builds her life totally around her man. She sacrifices important parts of herself, like her perspective, her values, her opinions, her voice, in order to be in relationship. Her theme is peace at any cost. When there is conflict she backs down, because to do anything else would be non-submissive.

More than a hundred years ago, the hymn "Have Thine Own Way Lord" was written. With apologies to the lyricist, I want to demonstrate how the dependent woman would sing this song.

Have thine own way, "dear," have thine own way.
You are the potter, I am the clay.
Mold me and make me after your will
While I am waiting yielded and still.

One of my clients voiced her dissatisfaction with this dependent position in a most creative way.

False Submission
1 Dependent Woman Lane
Lost Autonomy, Land of False Guilt!

Dear husband who believes in false submission,

I have been living in this fantasy world with you for over 12 years now. For your sake, I gave up my freedom, my personal life goals, and my personhood. I thought that by doing this I would be pleasing God and you. I allowed you to rob me of my identity, and I feel very angry at my choice. I have allowed you to strip me of my personal dignity and self-worth. I have hidden my talents and intelligence so as not to threaten you. I have not used my voice in our relationship.

While I know it will not happen overnight, with God's help, day by day, I am going to move out of this address to relate to you as a woman with this new address:

True Submission
1 Wholeness Circle
Interdependent, Evergrowing Place

With love,
Your wife.

Some women, perhaps as a reaction to the prison of dependence or as a result of a divorce, opt to become independent women. They are the captains of their ships. If anything, they become "antidependent". No one is going to tell them what to do. Mold them into someone else's image? No way! If there is any molding to do, the independent woman is going to do her own molding. Love may have meant that she was hurt, engulfed, abandoned, deprived, controlled, or abused. Whatever the reason, she has decided to be in control. If she fails she is certain that she will be controlled. Some independent women cherish a sense of entitlement. They honestly believe that life should just work out their way.

Not only is the woman who adopts the independent stance bound by her own smallness, she also makes herself God. Her version of that old hymn is,

I'll have my own way, (friend, God, spouse), I'll have my own way.
I am the potter, you are the clay.
I'll mold you and make you after my will
While you are waiting, yielded and still.

CHRIST DISPELS CONFUSION: INTERDEPENDENCE

Idolatry warps our relationships with each other. The dependent woman turns her significant other into her god; the independent woman becomes her own god. Jesus Christ came to earth to demonstrate a radically different style of relationship—interdependence. The interdependent woman has turned the control of her life over to Jesus Christ. He is the only one whose control doesn't destroy. She knows who she is because she knows whose she is.

Only in Jesus Christ do any of us find true equality. The game of one-upmanship is a downer for both sexes. The Apostle Paul writes, "There is neither Jew nor Greek, slave nor free, male nor female; for you are all one in Christ Jesus" (Galatians 3:28). The interdependent woman has no need to get an ulcer trying to prove that she is not inferior. Because she is free to be herself and because she has nothing to prove, she takes this stance: "I am a person of worth and dignity and so are you."

This woman is free to reinforce and intensify another's sense of personhood. She is also aware that each one of us is in need of a Savior. "For all have sinned and fall short of the glory of God" (Romans 3:23). She takes personal responsibility for her growth or lack of it; husbands and wives together are "heirs of the gracious gift of life" (1 Peter 3:7). Her salvation is not dependent on any other person but on her personal relationship with Jesus Christ. She will reject any suggestion that you must be a carbon copy of her or that she must be a carbon copy of you.

How exciting and life-changing to realize, as the interdependent woman has, that Jesus Christ's powerful presence is in each of us thanks to the Holy Spirit. Christ is in you and Christ is in me. Cookie-cutter Christianity is neither Christ's desire nor the interdependent woman's goal. Each of us reflects God's image in the context of our own personality and we each play a vital role in the Body of Christ (see 1 Corinthians 12). The interdependent woman believes that she is in this world to become all that God intends her to be, and that you are here to become all that God intends you to be. If she can reinforce your growth, her own will be renewed. Competition is out: equality is in!

This woman neither intimidates knowingly nor is she intimidated easily. Because she accepts herself as an ever-growing, changing, and developing individual, she sees herself and others as "in process." Differences don't threaten her. At times they may be irritating, but many times she views them as exhilarating.

Just as Jesus values each of us for who we are—human beings, highly significant and of great value apart from what we accomplish—so the interdependent woman values those in her life. She focuses on others' possibilities and potential, and then affirms them. She is not threatened by the good in others because she has also embraced the good in herself.

Because her security is a direct result of God's acceptance and forgiveness, the interdependent woman chooses to risk and be vulnerable.

Why? Because she has nothing to lose and because her God is still risking. Ultimately, we are God's greatest risk because He has chosen to reach out, love and minister to this world through us. We are not robots; God created us as human beings with the potential to deny or accept God's will for our lives.

I suppose the greatest risk many of us will ever face is being who we are. Many dependent women are utterly terrified by this risk because they cannot bear any conflict or rejection. Each of us takes a deep breath when we enthusiastically approach life as ourselves. After all, we are giving other people the power to hurt us. So why do we do it? Because our Master did it before us. Because it is the route to feeling totally alive.

Jesus was the initiator of vulnerability. He was open about His hurts, hopes, dreams and despairs. He was the initiator in our love relationship. In 1 John 4:19 we discover that "we love because he first loved us." Christ's life was transparent. The gospels are rich with examples of Jesus' willingness to let people get to know Him and understand Him. Perhaps one of the ways this is most evident is through Christ's freedom to express His emotions. Because He owned and expressed numerous emotions, we are today able to relate to Him and love Him. Here are just a few examples of Christ's vulnerability. He:

- Wept unashamedly at Lazarus death because he loved him (John 11:35–36).
- Showed surprise when met by lack of faith (Luke 8:25).
- Expressed indignance to His disciples (Mark 10:14).
- Rejoiced (Luke 10:21).
- Got angry at the Pharisees' hardness of heart (Mark 3:5).
- Grieved deeply over Jerusalem (Luke 19:41).
- Demonstrated compassion numerous times (John 11:33–38).
- Experienced feeling of loneliness (Matthew 26:40).

Jesus showed vulnerability because He knew we could never love a God we couldn't relate to.

How honest are you being with yourself? William Kinnaird writes, "Ironically enough, people who have come to grips with their own inadequacies and limitations frequently are more effective in caring for and supporting others."[2] In order to be vulnerable with each other we have to take off our rose-colored glasses and admit our selfishness. We have to stop pretending we are perfect. Only God is perfect. We also need to own up to our mistakes. We must not be afraid to say, "I was wrong," "I hurt," and "I love you."

Yes, vulnerability involves risk, but we can risk because we are loved. The interdependent woman is aware that Jesus Christ, who knows her better than anyone else does, also loves her the most. That knowledge frees her to risk.

Jesus Christ is the ultimate model of interdependence. One aspect of His interdependence was His willingness to be involved in relationships. In fact, He left heaven so that He, the creator God, could meet us where we are and get to know us intimately. He made Himself available to us to such an extent that He identified with our needs and even our temptations (see Hebrews. 2:17–18). Just as He enthusiastically entered the lives of the disciples at whatever stage they found themselves, so He enters our lives and encourages us to go for more. His love encourages us and sparks growth in us.

Jesus was able to receive help from others. In fact he was not afraid to verbalize His needs. As a result the Samaritan woman gave Him water to drink, and at Gethsemane, His disciples gave Him companionship until they fell asleep. He received a donkey on which to ride into Jerusalem and the gift of a meal from a repentant Zacchaeus, all because He asked for it.

In the midst of His relationships, Christ never lost sight of either His identity or purpose. He called people to repentance, to be responsible to make their own choices to follow him. He communicates clearly His love through His life and His words. Then He leaves our responses to us. Never are we Jesus' puppets.

Now we, as Christ's followers, find ourselves growing through healthy relationships. 1 John 4:12 says, "No one has ever seen God; but if we love each other, God lives in us and his love is made complete in us." The Christian life was not meant to be lived in a vacuum. God's Word encourages us to be involved in relationships. As we rub shoulders with each other we see the need to be committed to one another. Only in commitment to imperfect human beings can we follow in our Master's footsteps.

The very word "commitment" grinds on many eardrums. Yet only after we have committed ourselves to the God of love can we commit ourselves to care for others and identify with their various stages of growth. We choose to walk, as much as humanly possible, where they have walked, to laugh and weep with them, to be available to them, to be as gentle with them as Jesus Christ is with us. We demonstrate our willingness to be vulnerable by speaking the truth in love about ourselves when we are in relationship. I choose to back up my words with an authentic lifestyle. In relationships I am willing not only to give but also to express my needs honestly and receive from others.

We are one of the best means of getting God's life and love to others. In all of our relating, we must remember that our purpose is for Christ to be formed in you and in me (Galatians 4:19). If we find ourselves imitating anyone but Christ or pressuring someone else to imitate us, then we need to confess and readjust. We need to honestly share, with no inhibitions, what we see happening and together we need to get our friendship back to its original purpose—that Christ will be formed in both of us.

Love is the evidence that I am Christ's woman. Only through dependence on Christ alone will I find myself freed to be a most courageous lover who will not lose her identity through loving but will find her God-given purpose in loving.

ACTION STEP

In your journal respond to this question. From the perspective of who you are today as a woman, what would you say to the little girl inside you?

"Don't worry about being like someone else.
Make the most of who you are, of who God made you to be."

JANET CONGO

DISTORTIONS: CULTURAL INFLUENCES

A friend and I were admiring her son's aquarium when she made an observation that deeply affected me. She said, "I'm sure fish discover water last because they are surrounded by it and swim in it." I thought, *Wow, I wonder what I am unable to see because I am so immersed in it.* I had to admit that the water I most often fail to notice is the water of my culture. It permeates my world and as a result I swallow so many myths about my value as a woman. Most of the time I don't even confront or question these myths and find myself operating as if they were true. Maybe I'm a lot more like fish than I want to admit.

The Apostle Paul warns the Roman believers not to tolerate what is so pervasively familiar: "Don't become so well-adjusted to your culture that you fit into it without even thinking" (Romans 12:2, *The Message*).

The most destructive cultural myth goes against the notion that we are born into this world with value. The myth is performance-based, teaching that each of us has to prove our value by what we do instead of who we are.

Many competent, creative, educated, and attractive women struggle with feelings of emptiness, depression, and failure. We even condemn ourselves for those feelings. This steady diet of self-condemnation eats away at our self-esteem until we are left denying our very worth as a person. Is this what the Lord envisioned when He created woman? Definitely not! This comes as a result of swimming around in our cultural waters, swallowing its myths, and accepting them as truth.

Have you ever struggled with feeling less significant as a result of being single, or as a result of choosing to be a stay-at-home mom, or as a result of having a "lesser" career than someone else you know? If so, you have swallowed the myth that your value is determined by what you do.

IS MY VALUE BASED ON WHAT I DO?

God created us to be human beings, not human doings. I knew that truth and yet I stumbled into the trap of defining myself by what I did. It wasn't until I was absolutely miserable that I became aware of the water in which I'd been swimming.

Years ago I left my homeland of Canada so that my husband could pursue his dream. Dave had been accepted at the Rosemead School of Psychology, a graduate school of Biola University in Southern California. I had received the welcome news that Biola was interested in my teaching in the early childhood area. I was thrilled, as I had taught at the university level for seven years prior. After arriving in California, we enthusiastically set out to find a home. We soon settled into a new lifestyle and culture, confident of God's direction in our future.

Three months after I began teaching, I had to stop. It was Proposition 13 time and I was a Canadian. According to that legal document, I was taking a job away a U.S. citizen who needed work. Frantically, we appealed the decision with the Department of Immigration three times, only to receive the same answer. "No, Janet Congo cannot legally be employed in the United States of America."

We found ourselves facing a crisis. Dave was deeply involved in his doctoral program, we had a child to support and we had purchased a small home with much larger house payments than we were accustomed to in Canada. Dave possessed a student visa that entitled him to work 20 hours a week on campus, but any of you who have worked on a college campus know that means minimum wage! Because of our Canadian citizenship he could not qualify for American student loans. Neither could he qualify for Canadian loans because he was studying outside of Canada. What were we going to do to survive a five-year doctoral program?

I hit the pits. Not only was there phenomenal financial pressure, I also had to admit that my self-esteem had been tied into that prestigious university job—along with the nice little paycheck I received at the end of the month. From my beautiful office on the college campus I had always said that being a homemaker was the highest of all professions. However, now that I found myself forced to be a full-time homemaker, my self-esteem plummeted. Not only did I feel sorry for myself and afraid of what the future would hold, I felt very insecure about not being able to fit into the mold of the "successful" woman.

I responded by making an intellectual decision to be a superwoman. The Proverbs 31 woman would have nothing on me! She may have acquired her qualities over a lifetime, but I was determined to get them overnight. I struggled constantly to prove my worth. It got so bad that if I didn't have something concrete to show my husband and our son at the end of every day, I felt like a failure.

Externally, everything looked fine. The house was immaculate, the meals were nourishing and often gourmet, the children's needs were met and my husband was happy. But internally I was absolutely miserable. There was no time to cultivate my personal interests. I felt as though I lived constantly for everyone else's approval, under everyone else's control. I shudder even now as I recall this stage. I enjoyed very little. Nothing was ever quite perfect enough, on my part or anyone else's. And because I was so hard on myself it wasn't long until I was equally hard on others. Why couldn't they live up to my standards and expectations? This misery came as a direct result of believing that I had to prove my value or I was worthless.

IS MY VALUE BASED ON MY FINANCES AND WHAT I OWN?

Our society would answer "Yes!" Our world's idea of being acceptable is to prove our self-worth by our net worth. We acquire things and compare our possessions and finances to those of others.

Our slogans betray us. Where do we go when the going gets tough? You guessed it—we go shopping. Who wins at the end of life? You're right again, the one with the most toys. Could that possibly be true? No, our relatives win, since we can't take anything with us. A hearse never pulls a U-Haul® trailer.

I came face-to-face with the reality that I felt more valuable when I could buy new clothes and purchase new items. I had stopped teaching college to have our first child. I hadn't realized up to that point how much my self-worth was tied into receiving a paycheck every month. As precious as newborn babies are, I discovered that they do not score high in their ability to give mothers needed quantities of affirmation or financial remuneration.

My feelings were a little shaky when a friend would stop by at least three times a week wearing a cute little something she had just picked up at the store. My inability to handle being low woman on the buying totem pole drove a wedge into our relationship. When I swallowed this myth I confronted the blackness of my own jealousy. I was in bondage to other people's standards.

IS MY VALUE BASED ON WHO I KNOW?

If we hold to this philosophy we soon find ourselves using people to fulfill our own selfish ends. And it isn't long before we become a name-dropper. Sometimes even in our Christian circles the insinuation is made that God is particularly impressed by celebrities or by people who are trying to become celebrities. As a result we walk around either threatened by the status of other people or we become a threat to others.

Sometimes we even believe that if we're married, we have more status than someone who is single. How often are we tempted to believe that we aren't complete without a man? It's just a hop, skip and a jump from that false belief to believing that men make us more valuable and we, by ourselves, are somehow "half people."

That myth propels us to desperation if we don't happen to have a significant other. Many of us give up ourselves in order to be loved by a man. Unfortunately, a half-woman will only be attractive to a half-man. No man is capable of completing us. What we really need to find is a man and a half, but men don't come in that variety—so we're in big trouble. We end up battling a man who is expecting that we complete him at the same time that we are expecting to be completed.

IS MY VALUE BASED ON MY APPEARANCE?

Turn the pages of any fashion magazine on the newsstand, and you'll have to agree that the beautiful people certainly seem to get the most attention. Ordinary is not good enough; extraordinary is required. So we pursue fad diets, plastic surgery and extreme exercise routines.

The beauty propaganda begins when we are very young. Think

about those fabulous fairy tales we all enjoy. They reinforce the concept that the good girl is beautiful and the wicked girl is ugly. The ugly girl gets to relate with the furry animals in the forest. The beautiful one always gets her dream, usually in the form of a man or even a prince. But the story ends before we discover whether he turns out to be a dream or a nightmare!

The purpose of the billion dollar cosmetic industry is to persuade all of us that we'd benefit from a little help. The March 2001 issue of *Oprah* magazine carried a fabulous article entitled, "Blowing Our Cover." In an interview, Oprah revealed what it really takes to make a cover girl. As a result of a couple of dozen experts, lenses, light meters, wind machines, filters, mirrors, makeup brushes, curling irons, styling gel, trunks of wardrobe and makeup, Oprah was transformed. Her vulnerability and honesty warmed my heart. The author, Lisa Kogan, asked Oprah if she ever goes out in public prior to being transformed. "All the time," Oprah says laughing, "Years ago in Nashville, this woman starts following me around…Finally she says, "Oprah, is it you?" She continued on, "I thought so, but I couldn't imagine you'd come out looking like this!"[3]

You've got to love Oprah's willingness to be vulnerable. What a folly it is to compare ourselves to the flawless beauty on the magazine cover—who, by the way, had her hair styled by the same hairdresser still hovering in the wings to make certain that her "natural" look is sustained.

ACTION STEP

Have the cultural waters that you've been swimming in affected you? Take the time to reflect on these questions in your journal:

1. How do you feel about yourself at the end of a day when you have scheduled 10 things to accomplish and you haven't completed one?
2. If, for any number of reasons, you have chosen not to pursue a career outside your home at the present time, how do you feel when someone asks you what you do?
3. Do you feel more valuable when you are bringing home a paycheck?

4. Was there ever a time in your life when you chose not to entertain because your home wasn't furnished the way you wanted it to be? Explain.
5. Is there any way that you use shopping to change your mood or to counteract your sagging self-esteem?
6. In whose presence do you feel inadequate? Why?
7. Have you ever found yourself treating people differently if they were wealthy, attractive or had outstanding credentials?
8. In what ways have you been personally affected by the beauty propaganda that surrounds you?
9. What would you change about your physical appearance if you could?
10. How self-conscious do you feel when you are struggling with acne or when you are 10 pounds overweight?

THE EARNING MYTH FOSTERS A FANTASY MINDSET

When we contrast our appearance, accomplishments, friends, or possessions to others we make a comparison based in large part on fantasy. We have never walked in the shoes of those women and yet we compare ourselves to them. Whether we mean to or not, we compare our worst, of which we are most aware, to what we perceive to be their best. At that point, we're really comparing ourselves to a fantasy. Perhaps this is one of the reasons why soap operas and romance novels are so popular. Dissatisfied with our existence, we choose to live our lives vicariously through other people.

When we believe we are only worthwhile if we are beautiful, if we use the right products, if we know the right people, if we are successful, or if we are financially comfortable, we build self-image on faulty foundations. Subtly we find ourselves looking to other "significant" people to define for us what it means to be beautiful or financially comfortable, or what the right products are, who the right people are. A wealthy financier was once asked how much money he would need to be truly happy. His reply was, "just a little bit more."

When we swallow these faddish opinions, society loves us because we fit its mold. But what happens when the mold changes? Once again we experience rejection based on our performance because it is measured against someone else's standard. What insecurity results! This is a disastrously self-defeating process. We are pressured to achieve, and when we don't "succeed" we are immobilized by a crushing burden of failure and guilt.

One of the most sinister builders of faulty foundations is the secular media. Producers bombard women with the belief that our sense of fulfillment can only come outside of the home and that our brain is in neutral while we're at home. Has that indoctrination affected you? Women's magazines tell us how very easy it is to be completely fulfilled. All we need is a little organization, efficiency, and a highly competent housekeeper to run our homes while we pursue our careers. A nanny doesn't hurt either!

Picture this model mother as described by the secular media. Her alarm rings at 5:30 A.M. and she leaps out of bed, ready for another meaningful day. She feeds and dresses the baby, puts a load of laundry in the machine and enjoys a leisurely bubble bath while her toddler sleeps a little longer. (The authors of these "motivational'" articles never tell us what the baby is doing while the mother is having a leisurely soak!)

While the clothes are in the dryer, the model mother prepares a marvelous new dinner recipe clipped from a magazine the day before. When the toddler awakens she somehow manages to bathe and dress him, make the beds, read the morning paper, and get herself dressed in her classic blue lint-free business suit. She serves a nourishing and appetizing breakfast to her family.

At precisely 7:45 the babysitter arrives. Mother has 15 minutes to give her directions for the day, play with the children and kiss them good-bye before leaving the house. She looks well put together and ready to face the business world.

She takes on the challenges of the business day with enthusiasm and competence because she knows that things are being handled well at home. Before she leaves the office at night she takes the time to redo her makeup and dab on a little fragrance. She's had a busy day, but she arrives home peaceful and fulfilled in a relaxed frame of mind, anxious to have quality time with her children and her husband. After a beautiful, candlelit dinner together and story time with the children, she puts her contented, happy, sweet-smelling offspring to bed. Then she changes into "a little something" and prepares for an exciting, intimate exchange with her husband. They relax together and then she goes to bed feeling sexy enough to initiate a love–making time. She feels oh, so fulfilled.

The articles tell us it is quite possible to juggle motherhood, marriage, a career and your own sense of autonomy. Only after this fantasy bombards us long enough do we realize the impact it has had: we have extreme difficulty hearing what God is really saying. We fail to realize that we have value apart from whether we stay at home or work outside the home, apart from the wardrobe or finances we have, apart from who we know or how we look.

THE EARNING MYTH RESULTS IN A YEARNING MENTALITY

When we believe that we must prove and earn our value, we constantly seek and yearn for approval and validation from other people. We give them tremendous power over us. As a result, we learn to take care of others' needs at the expense of our own. We become pleasers who find it extremely difficult to accept our humanity with its weaknesses and limitations. When we don't believe in, accept, and love ourselves, we will be on the lookout for another human being who will do that for us. We become dependent on that person's validation. We try harder and harder. As a result, we are easily manipulated and exploited.

We say, "Yes" to projects that others want us to do, not because we are being true to ourselves and to our passion, but because we want to be liked. We live to be approved of. Identity gets tied up in being "nice" and not rocking anyone else's boat. At the same time our own unrealistic expectations bombard us. The "could have," "should have," "would have," and "if only" phrases haunt us day and night. We constantly feel like we haven't done well enough or been good enough.

This constant self-deprecation leads to the condition I call "ingrown eyeballs." It's as if we have a radar for negativity and weakness. We're like a cat chasing its tail; as hard as the cat tries she can't get what she's after.

One woman was overhead saying of another, "She has a large circle of friends. Too bad it doesn't include herself." It's as if we carry a gigantic magnifying glass in our head. It enlarges our every negative and exposes our every flaw. It isn't long until we start to believe that God has the same standards as our culture. We believe that our performance can increase or decrease His love. We start to believe that we have to earn His favor too. We project the world's value system onto God and we distort His Word. We have just enough religion to make us truly miserable. We find ourselves constantly falling short of the mark. The god of our own making is always pointing out our failures, expressing his disappointment and condemning us. We are doomed. We are miserable.

Have you been chasing someone else's standard and assuming it was God's requirement? Our culture sees our self-worth as a function of our accomplishments, accumulations, and attractiveness. The quest for more to fill up our emptiness can be as addictive as any drug. Enough is never enough. We spend every waking moment yearning for more, feeling entitled to it, and feeling resentful that someone else may have it. Why them? Why not me?

When feelings of insecurity were overwhelming me as a result of the Department of Immigration's decision, I was offered the opportunity to lead a women's Bible study at the Crystal Cathedral. I accepted the position, not because I wanted to know more of my wondrous Lord or because of any concern for hurting women, but because I believed this was the way I could prove I was worthwhile. I'm so glad I took on that assignment. Had I not, I might never have made the time to be in the Word—there were just too many fires to put out, too many ways to prove to others that I was indispensable. As a result of my study of the Word of God I began to comprehend just how different God's standards were from those our Western culture promotes. It was around that time that my friend made her insightful comment about fish. All of a sudden, something clicked inside me. I became aware of the influences that I had been tolerating in my life, myths perpetrated by the culture I lived in, myths that were destructive to my self-esteem. Have you also been swallowing lies that have left you uncomfortable in your own skin and that have added to your misery? It is time to differentiate between God's standards and those of our culture. It is time to abandon some distortions and instead embrace reality as God sees it. Our very security depends on it. After all, love has branded you.

Part Two

REALITY

WHAT IS REALITY?

Many of us could have written this letter, which I received in the mail.

> November 10, 1986
> Dear Jan:
>
> Having just come from hearing you speak, I wished to write to you and confirm the work the Lord has begun (Philippians 1:6) in you and through you …
>
> My husband and I are "leading" couples from a large church. We have the family that others would evaluate and say we "have it all" (actually, we do, we've carelessly abused the blessings)! You were part of a process that reached in and touched our hearts—warmed and encouraged us to try again in the process called life …
>
> I came from nowhere—at two placed in adoption—taken by a woman who married four times by the time I was in first grade. Someone way back there molested me and then she and my new "father" abandoned me with his mother and I was left alone, again. Two years or so passed, she came back and off we went to a real family. I received and loved Jesus (as we were dumped off in a Sunday School each Sunday). About the same time, my "father" became a lover, a molester, rapist, and destroyer. He hated and despised me and beat me because of it. Then, as usual, he accused and very much convinced me (as I've only recently realized) I was not only bad, but I was evil. I took on my "father's" image and God took on my "father's" image. I lost my stepmother (she did-

n't protect me and allowed the evil. I lost a "father" and I lost God.) I was 10 years old.

Jan, you won't remember this lady in burgundy, dressed and tailored, hair in place and smile on my face—but you looked me directly in the eyes and said, "Ladies, God loves you!" You said it with such certainty and conviction. Then you said it took you 33 years to experience that love. All day you spoke and rekindled the hope of the possibility that I could reach out to God and He would not look upon me with my child's perception of disgusted eyes.

Oh what hope and what anxiety to even hope that I have value. You wished to give me a gift—love/God/value. … As your eyes met mine, Jan, I felt a pain in my heart—perhaps the sword of God, cutting away at the fear and bitterness. I dared hope a little more and dared to share this with my husband. I am committed to return to therapy and try to trust a Christian woman who says she wants to help.

Thank you for loving and obeying God; because of your life I've been given another ounce of courage not to just exist, but to truly live …

From a child who thought she wished to die and who is full of anxiety even now.

What if there is love?

Linda

November 16, 1986

Dear Linda,

There is love.
There is hope.
There are possibilities.
There is empowerment.
There are good people, and
There is God.

Because Christ heals,
Janet Congo

How I see God directly affects how I see myself. So many of us have picked up limiting beliefs about ourselves either because of another's cruel demeaning words, because of our culture's or other peoples' pressure, or because of our own negative self-talk. That gets in the way of our understanding God's perspective of us. We must learn to see ourselves through God's eyes. But can we trust God? Who is He anyway?

In order to believe what God says about our value, we must trust the Source. Jesus is the human manifestation of the heart and character of God. Jesus' words and actions reveal four characteristics of God that are crucial to our self-esteem. God is our pursuer, our Father, our lover, and He wants to be our Lord and Savior.

GOD IS MY PURSUER

So many of Jesus' stories about God's love express a steadfast determination. In Luke 15, He tells of a woman who searches all night until she finds a valuable coin, and then of a shepherd who leaves his flock to hunt in the darkness for one lost sheep who has wandered away. Jesus continues with a third parable of the lost son who left home and blew his inheritance in a faraway country. That story demonstrates God's character in such an amazing way. The following is the Congo version of the prodigal "daughter":

There was a man who had two daughters. The younger one came to her father one day. She stomped her feet and said in a demanding manner, "Father, give me the money from my inheritance. I don't want to wait until you're dead so that I can begin to live. I want to stand on my own two feet. I'm tired of the restrictions in this home. I'm going to go away to the big city and prove that all of your fears are groundless. I'm only young once. I owe it to myself. I'm going with or without your permission."

So the Father sadly gave his daughter her share of the inheritance.

In a few hours, the daughter got her belongings and headed for the lights and glamour of the big city. She carried with her all the fantasies of youth and all her expectations that people would welcome her with open arms because of her beauty and talent.

For a time it felt like heaven. She was free of her parent's restrictions. She was able to purchase incredible clothes. She felt so glamorous with all her expensively labeled clothes. Somehow the clothes seemed to increase her value. She visited hot singles bars. She found young men quite attentive, especially when she bought them drinks and promised them something more! The first time she got into bed with a stranger, it felt exhilarating and naughty. The taboo helped her feel so sexy.

The next morning was awful. Shame consumed her, but after a few chapters from a romance novel, she was ready to fall in "love" again.

She ate at the most fashionable restaurants. She had a beautifully furnished apartment. She went for the most handsome and flashy men. She even succeeded in getting her name in the gossip columns periodically. She felt proud that she could keep up with the "wildest" of them. She thought her dad was all washed up, an "old fogey." This was real living!

For months she lived the wild life in the fast lane. But it couldn't go on indefinitely. Her inheritance wasn't going to last forever. As her finances dwindled, a gnawing fear started to eat away at her. She was getting tired too. The girls in the singles bars seemed younger every night. The guys were addicted to the initial rush of the relationship. They were constantly on the lookout for someone new to conquer, and there always seemed to be someone new.

Still she hoped that someone would fall in love with her and break out of his pattern of addiction. She thought she'd found the man of her dreams only to discover he was married and had no intention of leaving his wife.

She was sure she'd feel better about herself if she had a career.

Anyway there were those blasted finances! She moved out of her lavish apartment into a much smaller one. Her fair-weather friends ridiculed her.

Her so-called friends left in search of more excitement. She knocked on many doors, sent out (it seemed to her) hundreds of resumes, faced many rejections and finally ended up with a job as a Girl Friday at a law firm.

She knew in her heart of hearts that she was fortunate to have the job, and she committed to do anything she needed to keep it.

Things went along well for a couple of months. Then one evening as she was leaving work, one of the partners asked if she would come into his office to discuss a project. She was raped! Then she was threatened that if she squealed she would lose her job. She stumbled back to her small apartment that night, hot tears of anger flowing down her cheeks. Her body trembling and aching, all the while feeling so violated. She knew she needed the job. She didn't have many skills, she desperately needed the money, and she couldn't count on any of her friends to help. She bought a bottle of hard liquor and drowned her humiliation in it.

The next morning she could hardly drag herself out of bed. Her head throbbed. Her body was on fire. Her conscience burned. Her self-respect was squelched. She had to drink some more just to get up her nerve to go out into the world.

It happened again and again and again. At first she abhorred it, then she allowed it, and finally she began to desire it. After all it was the only intimacy she knew even if it was a counterfeit one.

The lawyer introduced her to a little white powder that made her feel good. It enabled her to forget, if only temporarily and Lord knows she needed to forget. It wasn't long until a large portion of her salary was used not to pay rent, but to help her feel good.

One day she came into the office to discover that a new "Girl Friday" had been hired—one with a gorgeous figure, beautiful hair, and a fabulous wardrobe. She went in to see her boss. He called her a "slut" and fired her on the spot.

She spent all her salary on white powder that day.

Now there was no more money. What was she to do?

There was only one way she could get money to survive and she knew it. She could sell her body, she'd already sold her soul. That way she could get back at the men who had taken advantage of her. If she got a disease, she'd pass it on to some of them.

So she tried it once, but almost in spite of herself she began to think, "The cleaning women in my parents' home have more pride than I do. They have a roof over their head and food in their stomachs. They have self-respect. They can look at themselves in the mirror." She thought, "Here I am, selling my very body, fast on my way to becoming a statistic. I'm going to go home and beg my father's forgiveness."

So she got up—her dreams shattered, her self-esteem squelched, her expectations dashed, and her hopes crushed. She had come to the absolute end of her "ideal" self and she was finally willing to face the truth. She started on her journey home.

But while she was still a long way off, her Father saw her coming and was filled with compassion for his lost daughter. He ran to this thin, trembling, tired young woman. His eyes were filled with love, not judgment. With forgiveness, not conditions; with acceptance, not condemnation. He threw his arms around her and kissed her. Tears cascaded down her cheeks.

"Oh, Daddy, she cried, "I've sinned against God, against you, and against myself. I've done evil things beyond your wildest imaginations. I'm no longer worthy to be called your daughter I've brought disgrace to your name. I'm worse than nothing. I'm a failure."

But the father said to his maids, "It's celebration time! Quickly, without delay, bring the most beautiful white gown and put it on her. Put one of the family heirlooms around her neck and new shoes on her feet. Bring the best of everything I have. Let's have a feast and celebrate. My daughter who was lost is found."

In this story, God is the ever-watchful father. His love pursues us. He isn't focused on duty, a desire to punish, or to get revenge. The Almighty God of the universe throws a party upon hearing the news that we have finally come to the end of our own adequacy and acknowledged our need of Him.

GOD IS MY FATHER

In spite of stories like the one you just read, the word "father" means many different things to different people. No matter how wonderful or how wicked your earthly father was, God bears no resemblance to him. Many of us have difficulty understanding or even desiring a relationship with God, the Father, because of the pain we experienced at the hands of our earthly father.

Jane was severely beaten as a child. She faced more anger than affection from her father. Rarely, if ever, were words of love or affirmation expressed. It was incomprehensible to her that God, her heavenly Father, could be anything but an angry and vengeful figure—a replica of her earthly father.

Jane's eyes were blinded to God's love, grace and forgiveness until she asked the Holy Spirit to walk back through her past with her. Likewise, it wasn't until she was willing to forgive her father (even though this parent still justifies his behavior) and search the Scriptures for clues as to what God's character is really like, that her life began to change. Over a period of time she was finally able to replace her personal experience of "father" with the Scripture's definition of God as Father.

It is essential to our belief in a loving God that we differentiate between an earthly father and our heavenly Father. We must begin the process of forgiving our father for the choices he made that left us wounded. We do this not to let him off the hook nor necessarily to reconcile, but to free ourselves from the burden of hate. If we refuse, than any time we hear God referred to as "Father," feelings of bitterness, repulsion, anger and perhaps even hate will overwhelm us. With a heart full of disdain for an earthly father, it is impossible to turn towards our loving, heavenly Father with adoration, worship, obedience and praise. We will find it impossible to believe that God values and loves us. All we will be able to focus on is our perception of God's "disgust" and our guilt over failing to let go of our woundedness.

ACTION STEP

Is it possible that you have thoughts, ideas and concepts of God that are unworthy of Him because of your painful associations with the word "father?" Write your thoughts down in your journal.

HE IS MY LOVER

God the Father's love is beyond human comprehension. Thankfully that hasn't stopped humans from attempting to describe this amazing love. I have found Dick Dickinson's paraphrase of 1 Corinthians 13:4–7 extremely helpful in redefining what God the Father's character is like:

> Because God loves me, He is slow to lose patience with me.
>
> Because God loves me, He takes the circumstances of my life and uses them in a constructive way for my growth.
>
> Because God loves me, He does not treat me as an object to be possessed and manipulated.
>
> Because God loves me, He has no need to impress me with how great and powerful He is because He is God. Nor does He belittle me as His child in order to show me how important He is.
>
> Because God loves me, He is for me. He wants to see me mature and develop in His love.
>
> Because God loves me, He does not send down His wrath on every little mistake I make of which there are many.
>
> Because God loves me, He does not keep score of all my sins and then beat me over the head with them whenever He gets the chance.
>
> Because God loves me, He is deeply grieved when I do not walk in the ways that please Him because He sees this as evidence that I don't trust Him and love Him as I should.
>
> Because God loves me, He rejoices when I experience His power and strength and stand up under the pressure of life for His name's sake.
>
> Because God loves me, He keeps working patiently with me even when I feel like giving up and can't see why He doesn't give up on me, too.
>
> Because God loves me, He keeps on trusting me when at times I don't even trust myself.
>
> Because God loves me, He never says there is no hope for me, rather, He patiently works with me, loves me and disciplines me in such a way that it is hard for me to understand the depth

of His concern for me.

Because God loves me, He never forsakes me even though many of my friends might.[4]

ACTION STEP

Answer this question in your journal:

Which of these statements describing God's love has the most meaning for you? Why?

MY LORD AND SAVIOR

Your belief in Jesus Christ as Lord and Savior hinges on the death and resurrection of Jesus Christ. History bears witness that Jesus was crucified on a hill called Mount Calvary. There God's son was stripped, beaten, spat on, struck in the face, garlanded with thorns, taunted, and hung on a cross to die. Why? Because Jesus knew that in God's plan, He must die in order for you to live eternally with God. Sin must be punished. Since none of us can live a sinless life, Christ willingly took the punishment for our sin on Himself. Christ really was born to die so that we could live eternally with God.

Paul writes powerfully to the Colossian believers about what Christ's death accomplished: "Once you were alienated from God and were enemies in your minds because of your evil behavior. But now God has reconciled you by Christ's physical body through death to present you holy in his sight, without blemish and free from accusation" (Colossians 1:21–22).

The God of the universe loves you. Because of what Jesus did on Calvary, He accepts you and views you as perfect. You are, from this moment on, dressed in Jesus' righteousness. You come from greatness!

Because of Christ's death on the cross, you can stand before God unafraid and secure in the knowledge that you are His child and that you will spend eternity with a Holy God. Philip Yancey writes these powerful words: "The cross redefines God as One who was willing to relinquish power for the sake of love. Power, no matter how well-intentioned, tends to cause suffering. Love, being vulnerable, absorbs it. In a point of convergence on a hill called Calvary, God renounced the one for the sake of the other.[5]

Thankfully Jesus didn't stay on the cross. Death didn't have the final word. According to all four gospels, women were the first witnesses of Christ's resurrection. Since Jewish courts did not accept the testimony of female witnesses, this is an amazing fact of history. Even the words of Mary Magdalene and Mary the mother of Jesus did not persuade the disciples. Nor did the empty tomb persuade them. What radically transformed the disciples' belief system was Christ's multiple visitations to each of them. Jesus overwhelmed the witnesses' faith: anyone who saw the resurrected Jesus lost the freedom of choice to believe or disbelieve. In six weeks, Jesus established His identity for all time.

What was the result? Cowardly, unstable, and unreliable followers were transformed into fearless witnesses to the reality that Jesus had overcome even death.

Women who had no voice experienced having the first and last word. Men and women were never the same again. This same Jesus Christ desires to be your Savior and Lord. He wants to transform your reality and your identity with His powerful love. Do you dare to believe that the scriptural account is true? Is Jesus who He said He is?

WHAT DOES JESUS SHOW ME ABOUT GOD?

God gave us Himself in the form of a person. Jesus is God's way of letting us grow in our understanding of God's heart and character. Only through Jesus Christ can we as women discover our sole source of freedom. We are free only when bound to this loving God, who cared enough about each one of us to send His only begotten Son so we would have a "fleshed out" picture of what He is truly like. Let's examine the Scriptures together to discover what Christ showed us about God, our heavenly Father.

> He is the loving, concerned Father who is interested in the intimate details of our lives (Matthew 6:25–34).
>
> He is the Father who never gives up on us (Luke 15:3–32).
>
> He is the God who sent His Son to die for us though we were undeserving (Romans 5:8).

He stands with us in the good and bad circumstances of our life. (Hebrews 13:5).

He is the ever-active Creator of our universe. (1 John 1:3)

He died to heal sickness, pain and grief (Isaiah. 53:3–6).

He has broken the power of death (Luke 24:6–7).

He gives all races and sexes equal status (Galatians 3:28).

He is available to us through prayer (John 14:13–14).

He is aware of our needs (Isaiah 65:24).

He has created us for an eternal relationship with Himself (John 3:16).

He values us (Luke 7:28).

He doesn't condemn us (Romans 8:1).

God values and causes our growth (1 Corinthians 3:7).

He comforts us (2 Corinthians 1:3–5).

He strengthens us through His Spirit (Ephesians. 3:16).

He cleanses us (Hebrews 10:17–22).

He is for us (Romans 8:31).

He is always available to us (Romans 8:38–39).

He is a God of hope (Romans 15:13).

He provides a way to escape temptations (1 Corinthians 10:13).

He is at work in us (Philippians 2:13).

He helps us in temptation (Hebrews 2:17–18).

He wants us to be free (Galatians 5:1).

He is the final Lord of history (Revelation 1:8).

As if that isn't wonderful enough, the writer of the first chapter of Hebrews tells us these things about Jesus Christ:

He is greater than any human prophet (vv. 1–2).

He is God's Son (v. 2).

He is the heir of all things (v. 2).

He created the world (v. 2).

He is Himself God (v. 3).

He upholds all things (v. 3).

He cleanses us from sin (v. 3).

He sits at the right hand of the Father (v. 3).
He is greater than the angels (v. 4).
He bears the name of Son (v. 5).
Angels worship Him (v. 6).
He is the eternal God (vv. 8–9).
His throne is forever (v. 8).
He is the ruler of the coming age (vv. 10–12).

The most important question each of us must answer is, "What do I believe about God?" In these verses do you find the condemning judge ready to zap you if you step out of line? No! That god is a figment of an overactive perfectionist streak and the result of poor teaching. This is not the picture of God presented through and by Jesus Christ.

Our God is for us. Praise His Holy name! The God who is beyond us and above us chooses to live with us in Jesus Christ. The wonder of it all! Henrietta Mears said:

"Jesus is
God's mouth speaking God's message
God's eyes seeing our need
God's ears hearing our cry
God's mind knowing our troubles
God Himself in human form come to bring us God."[6]

When we get to know the Jesus of the Gospels, our perspective about God will be transformed. Philip Yancey puts it this way: "Because of Jesus, I must adjust my instinctive notions about God.... Jesus reveals a God who comes in search of us, a God who makes room for our freedom even when it cost His son's life, a God who is vulnerable. Above all, Jesus reveals a God who is love.[7]

WHAT WILL MY RESPONSE BE?

It is this same heavenly Father who invites us to come to Him by faith, believing that He will accept us, as we are, into His family. We don't have to earn His acceptance on the basis of our performance, our acquaintances, our possessions, our beauty or our marital status. In

John 3:17 we learn that God didn't come into this world to condemn the world but to save and free the world.

It is this same God who sees us as highly significant and greatly loved even though He knows we are fallen women. If you had been the only person on the face of this earth, God would have sent His Son to die for you. You are that valuable to Him, that precious to Him.

Have you asked this Jesus, the risen Christ, to be your personal Savior? Have you exchanged your concept of an earthly, imperfect father, for the scriptural description of God as a loving, perfect Father? If you choose to begin with a God of love, God will give you the right to become His child (John 1:12–13). Without Jesus demonstrating to us God's heart and character, all we as humans could do is tremble at the Unknown One and project our own human tendencies onto Him.

Because of Christ, we understand on a profoundly human level that God is alive, active, and present. We can run from Him, close our eyes to Him, resist Him and numb ourselves to His influence, but God's love remains. We are still the apple of His eye.

ACTION STEP

In your journal write Jesus a letter of thanks. Tell Christ how your understanding of God's heart and character has been increased because Jesus lived on planet earth. Then tell God what you personally are going to do with His Son, Jesus Christ.

Interdependency is unattainable unless we see God, our heavenly Father, as a loving Holy God. It is terribly difficult to give love unless you have been the recipient of love. Are you grounded in the safety of God's love?

WHY DOES MY VIEW OF GOD MAKE A DIFFERENCE?

Benjamin Zander, the conductor of the Boston Philharmonic Orchestra and professor at the New England Conservatory of Music, has a most unusual approach to grading his students. He gives each of his highly talented and gifted graduate students an "A" for the course if in the first two weeks of the class they will write him a letter which begins like this:

> Dear Professor Zander:
> I got my "A" because …

Using as much detail as possible, they must spin a story of what happened to them during the class that is in keeping with the extraordinary grade. They must place themselves in the future, looking back. They are to report on their acquired insights and their attained milestones. What he is most interested in is who this student has become by the end of the class. He wants them to report their attitudes, feelings, and worldview. His words are, "This "A" is not an expectation to live up to, but a possibility to live into."[8]

His hope is that each student will fall passionately in love the person they are describing in the letter. One of Dr. Zander's students wrote the following letter to justify her "A":

> Dear Mr. Zander,
> I got my "A" because I had the courage to examine my fears and I

> realized that they have no place in my life. I changed from someone who was scared to make a mistake in case she was noticed to someone who knows that she has a contribution to make to other people, musically and personally … . Thus all diffidence and lack of belief in myself are gone. So too is the belief that I only exist as a reflection in other people's eyes and the resulting desire to please everyone. … I understand that trying and achieving are the same thing when you are your own master—and I am.
>
> I have found a desire to convey music to other people, which is stronger than the worries I had about myself. I have changed from desiring inconsequentiality and anonymity to accepting the joy that comes from knowing that my music changes the world."
>
> GISELLE HILLYER[9]

When I first heard of this amazing grading system, I was struck with a transformative insight. This is what Jesus Christ has done for every person on planet earth. He has given us an "A" for life.

A SIGNIFICANT CREATION

In Psalm 8 we discover that we, as part of the human race, are the highest of God's created beings. With a sense of awe we realize that we have been made a little lower than the angels and crowned with glory and honor. Without God we would be just dust, for God breathed His very breath into dust to give us life (Genesis 2:7). As a result of reading Genesis 1:26, we are overwhelmed at the tremendous trust God committed to each of us when He gave us dominion over our part of the world.

A VALUED FEMALE

God not only sees us as highly significant people, He also affirms our value as women. Jesus Christ, the creator God, left the glory of heaven to willingly live and die on this earth because of His great love for people—male and female, slave and master, Jew and Greek. The culture he entered differentiated between male and female to such an extent that males were really the only sex granted a sense of personhood. Females were less than people—things—to be used by men for their pleasure.

According to the historian Josephus, the women of Jesus' day faced terrible prejudice. Jewish men prided themselves with the "spiritual truth" (taught in the Talmud) that women were inferior. Yet these same men used women in polygamous relationships and for prostitution. Into this sinful, arrogant world came Jesus Christ. Here was a radically different rabbi who affirmed women in astonishing ways. He treated women as valued persons. He took them seriously. He affirmed their intellectual capabilities by teaching them the Scriptures. He met their social needs by being their friend. He ministered to their emotional needs by meeting them where they were. He used everyday examples of women in His teaching; He listened to them, spent time with them and trusted women to be the first witnesses of the Resurrection. He offered salvation and healing to women as well as men.

God chose to have His Son be dependent on a woman for His birth, care and nurture. In the fourth chapter of John we find Christ giving the first revelation that He was the Messiah to a woman. He regularly taught women the Scriptures and was not afraid to hold a conversation in public with a woman. In Jewish tradition a woman was not permitted to bear witness, but Jesus' words after the resurrection to a woman were "go and tell my disciples."

Our Savior has affirmed us as persons. We are women who have been freed by Jesus Christ our Lord and we play a vital role in our world. Since our Savior treats us as people with dignity, can we treat ourselves as anything less?

A DIVINE ORIGINAL

God has placed tremendous value on our personhood. We are divine originals! Scripture teaches that we have been created in the image of the creator God (Genesis 1:27). Even though we do not fully comprehend the wonder of being made in God's image, each of us is aware of an inborn need to be creative and to make a difference. We are also born with a self-consciousness, a self-awareness that is non-existent in the animal kingdom. Our ability to moralize and think rational thoughts tie into the reality of what it means to be created in the image of our God.

A PRICELESS TREASURE

In today's world we are confronted daily with people willing to spend phenomenal amounts of money to buy one-of-a-kind-cars, vintage beverages, designer clothes, stamps—you name it. You and I might find it repulsive to spend so much money for those items, yet their value has absolutely nothing to do with our feelings. Their value is found in the hearts of men and women who are willing to pay such fantastic prices for them. In the same way our value lies not in how we view ourselves but in what God was willing to pay to redeem us. He paid dearly by giving Himself on Calvary (see John 3:16). Scripture also tells us that God loves us so much that He desires our company and wants to spend eternity with us (see John 14:2–3).

A HUMAN BEING

Are you often aware of your humanity, your frailties? Great! You are earthen and that's the way God meant it when He created you. Second Corinthians 4:7 explains why: "But we have this treasure in jars of clay to show that this all-surpassing power is from God and not from us." The beauty of Jesus becomes evident to those around us through our humanity. Is it really okay to be human? Yes! Why? Because Jesus the Creator God of the universe chose to be fully human.

Being human means we have mental and physical weaknesses; it means we experience energy limitations; it means we have needs and it means we have a mixture of emotions. Being human also means we have a need to love and be loved and to believe that we are significant persons. We will not be able to do everything we want to do or everything everyone else wants us to do. The great news is that God indwells our humanity so His beauty will shine forth in and through each of us.

A WOMAN IN NEED OF A SAVIOR

Jeremiah 17:9 says, "The heart is deceitful above all things and beyond cure. Who can understand it?" That's not a lot of fun to read, is it? But your feelings don't make it less true. I believe that Scripture is based on reality. Despite the clear teaching of the Bible to the contrary, we often try to convince ourselves and others that we really are pretty good.

I'm embarrassed to admit that when I first accepted Christ as my personal Savior, I didn't think God would have much work to do. After all, I was a pretty acceptable person by my standards. Was I ever surprised when I was confronted with God's standards!

The potential for every imaginable evil lies within each of us. We must not be fast with judgments, for given the same circumstances and temptations that others face, we, too, might succumb. I can't tell you how many times I have sat with a client who says, "I never imagined that I would do that." Mark writes of reality in Mark 7:21–22: For from within, out of [women's] hearts, come evil thoughts, sexual immorality, theft, murder, adultery, greed, malice, deceit, lewdness, envy, slander, arrogance and folly." The deceitfulness of our hearts is evident in our tendency to believe that the circumstances around us and the people in our lives are responsible for our responses to life. Adam blamed Eve and Eve blamed the serpent. "Any time we blame we choose to be lame." I learned this truth graphically some years ago. It was the day before Halloween and our five-year-old son Christopher and his friend Scotty were sitting on the porch swing. Their masks were pulled up on top of their heads, and they asked me for some cookies. Since it was only a few minutes before lunch I refused the request. As boys sometimes do, they helped themselves anyway. But in the process the metal lid of the cookie jar banged shut, giving me every indication of what was happening in the kitchen. (Every mother needs a metal lid on her cookie jar!)

When those two precious boys saw me coming toward them, they pulled their masks down over their eyes as if on signal. When they realized they had been trapped in their crime, Christopher blamed Scotty, and Scotty blamed Christopher. Needless to say, they both had a few moments to sit quietly and think about what they had done. But I was busy thinking, too. When there is something that needs confession in my life, do I rush to the Lord with it or do I pull down my mask? *Well, you know me, Lord; I've got a few faults. But a sinner? Let's not get too extreme now. Remember, Lord; I'm a good person.*

How often do I hide from the truth, believing that circumstances or other people are responsible for my actions? It is only when I can forgive others for their imperfections that I can forgive myself for mine.

Bruce Larson makes it exceeding clear where we stumble in our belief system: "If we really understand the Bible we have to revise our thoughts about heaven and hell. We think hell is for bad people and heaven is for good people. Actually, hell is for people who think they are good and heaven is for those who know how bad they are."[10]

Indeed we are deeply fallen women. "If we claim to be without sin, we deceive ourselves and the truth is not in us" (1 John 1:8). Each of us needs a Savior. For some reason we as women find it easier to believe in our fallen nature than to believe in the great value God ascribes to each of us. It is time for us to view the entire picture.

A FORGIVEN WOMAN

Christ had to die because there was no human way that I can meet God's perfect standards without Christ's divine intervention. With Christ's intervention I am acceptable to the Almighty God of the Universe.

> Yes, it is true that when you stand before the Lord to ask His forgiveness.
> Your dress is ragged and tattered because of ugly sins.
> Your hair is thickly tangled with the web of rebellion.
> Your shoes are torn and muddy by your past failures.
> But God never sees any of that!
> He sees you Holy.
> He sees you perfect.
> Because you are dressed in His righteousness.
> And He has covered you with the full-length cape of His love.
> He sees nothing else!
> Even when you explain how you really look underneath, he hears but He forgets forever.
> The dimension of His forgetfulness is as far as the East is from the West.
> And it endures past all eternity.
>
> (AUTHOR UNKNOWN)

A GREATLY LOVED AND ACCEPTED WOMAN

Calvary speaks to us of the immense value God attributes to us. Calvary demonstrates how deeply God loves us. There are no risks involved in God's love—none whatsoever. God accepts us in Jesus Christ, not because of our performance, but because of Christ's shed blood. The pressure is off. If we understand the meaning of grace, our defeats and failures should not cause us to turn away from God. Instead, they should cause us to turn towards Him in confession, praise and thanksgiving.

Ephesians 1:6 (KJV) points out that "we are accepted in the beloved." Because God is holy He can only accept perfection. Other than Jesus Christ, none of us is perfect. Regardless of how much effort we put into trying to become perfect, Christ alone is acceptable to God. Because we have been covered by Jesus' shed blood (see Galatians 3:27) and He indwells us, the Almighty God accepts us completely. We are not *just* forgiven sinners! We are not *merely* forgiven sinners. In God's eyes we are received and treated—accepted—as if we are Jesus, because of Christ's shed blood.

Exodus 11:4–6 contains a fantastic word picture of this truth. The death angel is going to pass over all the homes in Egypt, killing the firstborn in each home unless blood has been sprinkled over the door post of that home. What if some well-meaning, perfectionist woman had posted a list describing what a beautiful person she was, the activities all members of the family were involved in and the kindnesses they had done? The death angel would have struck that home bringing death and terror. It was the blood over the door post that made the family acceptable and so it is today. Christ's blood demonstrated the depths to which God was willing to go to get across His most important message: "I love you." Paul's words to the church at Ephesus describe that divine love. He writes: "And I pray that you (insert your name), being rooted and established in love, may have the power, together with all the saints, to grasp how wide and long and high and deep is the love of Christ, and to know this love that surpasses knowledge—that you may be filled to the measure of all the fullness of God" (Ephesians 3:17–19).

A woman who only believes she is forgiven focuses heavily on her performance rather than on her Lord. She must balance her gratitude for being forgiven with an understanding of being accepted as well. If we only believe we are forgiven, then we can be easily discouraged after confessing the same sin over and over again. What one of us hasn't experienced that? We begin to wonder if God hasn't lost patience with us. And it isn't very long until we question whether He'll accept us any longer.

We do not discover security in forgiveness alone. We only find security when we accept what Jesus Christ has done for us on Calvary and we understand His acceptance of us. When you have really understood this truth a communion service will no longer be a time for focusing on the awfulness of your personal sin. You will focus instead on God's fantastic grace and love. Much like the Israelites in Egypt, each of us gains acceptance in God's eyes only because of Jesus Christ's blood offering on our behalf.

A WOMAN WHO BELONGS

Because of what God the Father did by giving us His only begotten Son, I know the security that is a result of belonging. Based on the Word of God I know I am a child of God (see 1 John 3:1 and John 1:12); I have been accepted in the Beloved (Ephesians 1:6) and I am a new creature (2 Corinthians. 5:17). I have become part of a wonderful support group—the Body of Christ (1 Corinthians 12:27). When anyone in that group suffers I feel pain. When they rejoice, I rejoice, for they are the ones with whom I will spend eternity. I can be confident of this truth because in John 14:2–3, Jesus promises to prepare a place for those of us who believe in Him. When this life is over I can spend eternity with Him and with the other precious Christians I have learned to love here on earth.

A WOMAN WHO GIVES GOD PLEASURE

We gain acceptance in God's eyes only because of Christ's shed blood.

That is why I can confidently write this message: Regardless of your past mistakes or failures, if Jesus Christ is your personal Savior, God looks at each one of you and says, "You are my beloved daughter and I am pleased with you." It is time to take off the backpack of confessed guilt that weighs us down on a daily basis. We are forgiven women, accepted and loved by God.

One day I saw a two-sided poster and the potency of its message stopped me in my tracks. One side of the poster said: "World's view: I love you, I love you not." As you can guess there was a picture of a beautiful child picking the petals off a daisy. On the other side of the poster it said: "God's view: I love you, I love you, I love you …"

So it is. In God's eyes we are beautiful because of Jesus Christ's shed blood. It is impossible to love and enjoy ourselves until we have really learned to know and love our creator. When we love God we learn to love ourselves, from His perspective.

We believe three truths about ourselves—we are highly significant, deeply fallen, and greatly loved. Our true sense of worth comes with our awareness that we are loved and accepted unconditionally. This realization changes our focus from our mistakes and performance to the beauty of God's love and grace. We are freed from trying to please God and from living our life through others as the dependent woman does. We are also free to take off our masks and to stop pretending we can make it totally on her own as the independent woman does. The interdependent woman is the only person who is free to be herself because she is aware of who her wonderful God is.

A CHERISHED AND RESPECTED WOMAN

Not only do I give God pleasure when I trust His love, I also have a sense of being a person of value who is cherished and respected. Romans 5:8 shows me that God's love for me is not based on my performance, but on God's character. He cannot deny Himself:

"But God demonstrates his own love for us in this: While we were still sinners, Christ died for us." I have absolutely no possibility of earning God's favor, yet He sent His only begotten Son to earth to die for me. I know I am valued apart from anything I can do! I am now at peace with my God, who views me as His beloved daughter.

A TRANSFORMED WOMAN

As Christian women we sometimes fail to stress that we are transformed women. We are no longer just flesh people; we are now brand new spiritual people. Second Corinthians 5:17 gives us a radical revelation: "If [anyone] is in Christ, he [or she] is a new creation; the old has gone, the new has come!" We are not only forgiven sinners, but also transformed into new creations—God's very own children. First John 3:1–2 rings out: "How great is the love the Father has lavished on us, that we should be called children of God! And that is what we are! … Dear friends, now we are children of God." We, as transformed women, can now be transforming influences in our world.

A CONTRIBUTING WOMAN

God's love also fulfills my need for achievement. When Jesus was here on earth, willingly imprisoned in humanity, He acknowledged the impossibility of human beings living the Christian life apart from supernatural intervention. He knew He had dreams to give us that would be absolutely impossible without Him. The Father sent the Holy Spirit to do His work in each one of us. We have confidence, based on Philippians 1:6, that as long as we're willing, the Holy Spirit will keep us growing.

Why? In Ephesians 2:10 we discover that God wants us to accomplish good works—that is why He is at work in each one of us. The perfect plan involves women who are full of God Himself. Women who have the arms to hug the people in their world; the ears to listen to the joys and sorrows of their world; the hands to help those around them; the mind through which Christ thinks; and the mouth to speak words of comfort, wisdom and hope. I was created to make a difference in the lives of those I touch, just as Christ has made a difference in my life. Mother Teresa profoundly stated a simple truth. "It's not what we do that is so important, it is how much love we put into the doing."[11]

Accepting Jesus Christ as my personal Savior means I experience the security that results from knowing I belong to God and am a valuable and competent human being. Now I achieve, not to get a sense of adequacy, but out of an awareness of adequacy. "I can do everything through Him who gives me strength" (Philippians 4:13). One of my friends describes herself as a daughter of the King cleverly disguised as a Human Relations Professional.

ACTION STEP

In your journal answer this question.

After seeing yourself through God's eyes, how would you describe yourself?

Each of us needs to believe in the God who believes in us. Why? Because when we look into His eyes the reflection coming back at us is reality-based, affirming and transforming. Truly each of us has been given an "A." Are you willing to venture into the wonder of "A" living? What difference would it make in your life?

ACTION STEP

In your journal wrestle with this question.

If I truly believed in the core of my being that Jesus has given me an "A," what would I write in a letter to Him describing the person I have become over my lifetime?

"God gives each of us a possibility to live into!"

JANET CONGO

Part Three

REALITY BECOMES ACTION

THE 30-STEP ACTION PLAN

If you choose to, you can embark upon a personal journey towards interdependence. You can enroll in a training program that will launch you in the direction of personal confidence. Perhaps you would appreciate some company on your journey. Choose some women to support you who might like to begin their own journeys towards interdependence. Allow me to journey with you as well, to encourage and motivate you to begin your personal change process one step at a time.

Imagine that you were broke and I told you that I had deposited 10 million dollars into your checking account. What if you laughed at me, didn't believe me and walked away. What would happen? Absolutely nothing would happen. The only way to benefit would be to believe me and then take action on the belief by writing checks on that account.

God has, as it were, made an incredible deposit in our confidence account. He declares that we are priceless. He secures that affirmation by the death of His only begotten Son in our place. We are free to laugh at Christ's sacrifice and to walk away from it. But if we do, we lose. The only way to benefit is to adopt God's perspective of us and act on that belief by taking steps that affirm in reality what God has declared as truth.

I took the same 30 transformative steps in my own life. I have used these steps with women in retreat settings, in the counseling office, and in my role as a personal coach and mentor. This program lays out a step-by step plan leading to increased personal and relational confidence. Obviously you won't be cured of all your insecurities instantly.

Set your own pace and allow yourself all the time you need to work with each step.

Please stay focused on one step at a time. Don't read ahead. If you find yourself overwhelmed, slow down. Give yourself permission to go at your own pace. My goal is to give you the freedom to be you, which will allow you to bring all of who you are to your intimate relationships. As you faithfully work the program, you will walk away from both your people-pleasing, dependent tendencies and your self-centeredness and anti-dependence tendencies.

You will care about others, reach out to others and relate with others, but not at the expense of losing yourself. You will operate in accord with your personal passion rather than someone else's agenda. You will act out of choice, not compulsive compliance or angry reaction. Because you understand how much God loves and values you, you will begin to shine as a unique, precious human being. You were meant to leave an indelible print, as distinctive as those of your own fingers, on the lives of those within your circle of influence.

Your training program is about to begin. While you walk out these 30 steps you will develop an inner strength, an internal resilience, a sense of self-control, a moral fiber, and a determination to carry on no matter what. You will discover that strength isn't so much about developing our muscles as it is about developing our backbone—the backbone necessary to help you live the life you were truly meant to live.

The journey towards confidence and interdependence stretches out before you. I offer you my hand as you embark upon your journey.

> There are times in my life
> When I feel confused, lost and alone.
> When all around me seems to be in flux.
> I now trust that these times
> As uncomfortable as they feel
> Are really bridges to growth.
> So often I fight this truth internally.
> I struggle and try to recapture
> The security of the familiar—
> What appears to be "normal."

But almost in spite of myself
I emerge on the other side
With new understanding, new awareness.
And a new strength even in the broken places.
It seems necessary to go through the pain,
The confusion and the struggle
In order to grow and discover
More of the person who God created me to be.

JANET CONGO

STEP #1

Nurture My Spirit!

Max Lucado has written a magnificent children's book called, "You Are Special." (Crossway Books, Wheaton, Illinois, 1997). The first time I read it, tears came to my eyes. Since then I have watched it impact many others, young and not so young. Lucado writes about the Wemmicks, small wooden people who spend their days sticking beautiful gold stars or ugly gray dots on each other. Punchinello is one of the wooden people who has the misfortune of being the recipient of only ugly gray dots. He is so devastated by his standing in the Wemmick Kingdom that he rarely leaves his house.

One day he meets Lucia, a most amazing Wemmick. Stars and dots just fall off of her no matter how intentionally people try to stick them on her. Punchinello is in enough pain to risk speaking to Lucia. He asks her how it is that she doesn't have anyone's marks. She tells him that her stickerless state is a direct result of visiting Eli, the woodcarver, on a daily basis. Then she leaves little Punchinello alone to ponder whether Eli would even be interested in seeing a little Wemmick with so many gray dots. Finally his pain overcomes his fear and he goes to the woodcarver's shop.

Not only is Eli welcoming, he also knows Punchinello's name. Eli comments on Punchinello's gray dots. Punchinello says, "I didn't mean to, Eli, I tried really hard." Before the little wooden Punchinello could defend himself further, Eli tells him that he isn't at all impressed by what the Wemmicks think. Eli tells Punchinello only to be concerned by what he, Eli, thinks. According to Eli, Punchinello is pretty special.

Punchinello laughs and begins to point out all the things that he isn't. Then the little Wemmick stops himself and asks, "Why do I matter to you?" The answer comes back quickly, "Because you're mine. That's why you matter to me."

At that point Punchinello asks Eli why the stickers don't stick to his friend Lucia. Eli's reply is so wise: "Because she has decided that what I think is more important than what the Wemmicks think. … The stickers only stick if they matter to you. The more you trust my love, the less you care about their stickers." As Eli invites Punchinello to come back and visit him on a daily basis, he repeats his amazing message: "You are special because I made you. And I don't make mistakes." As the little Wemmick lets those words in, a gray dot falls to the ground.

What could be more security-producing than to know that the Creator of the universe is acquainted with me personally? He values me, understands me, infuses me with His life, accepts me, and loves me enough that He would allow His only Son to die in my place. What freedom comes with the realization that this same God has the power and desire to redeem all the experiences of my life! He longs to fill my emptiness with Himself, and He is preparing a place for me in eternity where there will be no feelings of inferiority, and no limitations.

SPEND TIME IN THE WORD (SEE 1 TIMOTHY 2:15)

Why? Not for the reason I used to read Scripture, which was to alleviate my feelings of guilt. You see, I knew it was something I was supposed to do if I was going to be a good Christian, so most nights I mechanically read a few verses, wondering all the while why so many people made so much of it. Personally, I found it quite a bore.

It wasn't until my guilt motivation was replaced by a love motivation that I discovered I wanted to be in cooperation with this Savior who loved me so much. I wanted to learn more about this holy, loving, forgiving, accepting Lord. I wanted the Holy Spirit to transform me into a loving, forgiving, accepting person.

We must be in the Word to discover our full potential. Just as electricity must run through a conductor, so the Holy Spirit works through the means God has provided—His Word. Have you asked the Lord to make you enthusiastic about meeting with Him daily? It's a daily battle for all of us, isn't it! Just as we don't get food for our bodies by looking at the unopened packages in the pantry, neither do we get spiritual food from an unopened Bible. We can attend three Bible studies a week, two seminars a month, all the church services available to us and hear others talk about the Word, but it won't nourish our spirits unless we personally take in the Word of God on a regular basis. Otherwise, we are limiting what the Holy Spirit can do in our lives.

The story is told of a husband whose wife died suddenly. He was left alone and broken to father their precious little daughter. The first Christmas after his wife's death, he decided to take the week off and spend it with his daughter. How he was anticipating that shared time. On the first morning the father rose excitedly, only to find that his daughter had shut herself in her room and would not come out until suppertime. The distraught father didn't know what to do. Should he leave her alone? Should he go in?

Finally Christmas morning arrived and under the tree was a package wrapped in newspaper, layers of tape and lots of ribbons. Triumphantly the little girl offered it to her beloved daddy. Upon opening it he discovered a pair of socks she had knit for him. "Daddy, this is what I was working on each day for you!" she exclaimed. Her daddy gathered her up in his arms, hugged her, and with tears rolling down his cheeks said, "Honey, I love the socks, they're beautiful. But all I wanted was time with you."

I wonder how often Jesus weeps over our busyness, our independence, our service for Him—longing to say to us: "My child, I just want time with you." Moffatt's translation of Isaiah 65:1 goes like this: "Ready was I to answer [women] who never … sought me. I cried out, 'Here am I,' to folk who never called to me."

Pause now and spend a moment centering all your thoughts on Jesus. Talk to Him about your desire to know Him better. Ask Him to make you enthusiastic about time alone with Him. He desires time with you, not to make you feel guilty, but rather so He can love you into your full potential as an interdependent woman. But beware. It could be habit forming!

SPEND TIME IN PRAYER (SEE 1 THESSALONIANS 5:17)

"Haven't you laid enough guilt trips on us?" asks the duty-motivated person. After all, when we're guilt-motivated we do pray. But we often ask God to put His "okay" on our plans and causes just before we fall into bed at night, exhausted. Then we fall off to sleep, relieved that we've done our duty.

The woman who is deeply touched by God's love for her prays because she is open to being changed. She admits her need for Christ's power. She prays in order to get a new perspective and to advance the cause of Jesus Christ.

We are in an exhilarating, creative partnership with the God of the universe when we pray. Prayer is not just a one-way communication with God where we tell Him all our needs and problems. It is also a time to adore, confess and thank our loving heavenly Father. It is a time to be completely honest with God. Are you angry with God? Confess it! He won't faint. He knows it already. Prayer is a time to ask questions and wait for His ideas and answers.

It is also a time to be silent and to open your mind so God's thoughts will flow to you. The psalmist writes,

> Show me your ways, O LORD,
> Teach me your paths;
> Guide me in your truth and teach me,
> For you are God my Savior,
> And my hope is in you all day long (Psalm 25:4–5)

God wants to shape our will and direct our steps. He enlarges our vision through prayer and gives each of us a dream that would be impossible without Him. Prayer opens up new possibilities in our world. Anne Ortlund uses an illustration comparing life to a funnel. The non-Christian woman enters at the wide end and finds that as she progresses through life, her options narrow until she finally finds herself at a dead end with no hope in sight. By contrast the Christian woman enters at the narrow end of the funnel, through belief in Jesus Christ as her Savior, and then finds all of life in its fullness opening up to her as she travels on her journey.

Do you feel a need to enlarge your vision or to change your perspective? Then cultivate your prayer life. Dream God's dreams for your life and your situation.

ACTION STEP

Set aside 15 minutes a day to meet with our Maker. During that time, look up one or two of the passages on the following chart. Get out your Sticky notes. On each one write the verse, rewording it with your name in it. Then write a summary sentence below it. For example:

Romans 15:7: "Christ accepted (your name)!
I, (your name), am accepted by God.

John 3:16
John 1:10–13
Isaiah 43:25
Genesis 1:27
Ephesians 1:6
Romans 15:7
Psalm 27:10
Luke 12:24
Isaiah 43:4
Isaiah 43:25
Psalm 18:19
Romans 8:1
Isaiah 54:10
Daniel 10:19
Ephesians 1:4
Isaiah 54:10
Hebrews 13:5
Philippians 2:13
Romans 8:31
Philippians 4:13
John 17:9

John 16:7
Ephesians 3:14–20
Jeremiah 29:11
Isaiah 61:3

If you would like to take this action step even further, write the same truth about the significant people in your life. Place your notes in places where you will read the truth multiple times each day.

Remember no one else will determine your value again. Your Maker, Jesus Christ, doesn't make any junk. Believe in the God who believes in you.

"Do not have your concert first and tune your instruments afterwards. Begin the day with God."

JAMES HUDSON TAYLOR[12]

STEP #2

Develop My Inner Strength Team

One of my favorite Bible stories is of the four men who carried their paralyzed friend on a stretcher to Jesus. When the friends got to the house where Jesus was teaching they found it so crowded that they had to come up with Plan B in order to get close to Jesus. They climbed up the stairs on the side of the house and carried their friend to the roof. Persistently they dug through the clay roof right above Jesus' head. Can you imagine what a distraction they created for those inside attempting to listen to the Master's every word? Apparently the four friends didn't care. They were on a mission. Public opinion didn't count. They were bringing their friend to Jesus. They dug a hole large enough that they could lower their paralyzed friend on that stretcher right down in front of the Master.

Do you have four people in your life who would carry you on a stretcher to Jesus in your moment of crisis? If even one person can say, "I'll be there for you," it changes everything. It is the devastating loneliness in the face of life's overwhelming realities that terrifies and petrifies us.

> People can't fight our battles or make our decisions, but they can comfort us, challenge us, encourage us, teach us and hold us accountable to grow. So many of our battles have to be fought essentially alone and often in the dark. But it is reassuring to know that we have people in our cheering section. People who believe in God, believe in us and who remind us of how God sees us. It has been said that,

"God has put us here not to see through each other, but to see each other through."[13]

We all need a cheering section. Our daughter Amy was born at four in the afternoon on the day our support group met. These precious people arrived at the hospital at 6:30 P.M. and prayed over our little girl. Another time someone in our group was going through a season of intense pain. Each member provided food for her and brought little homemade gifts all wrapped up. When the pain was terribly intense she had the joy of opening one of the presents and feeling loved and cared for.

Then there are the goals we share with each other. In our particular group we split up into pairs. We exchange our goals, agree to pray over each other's goals daily, phone each other at least once a week and hold one another accountable for personal growth. Given that kind of support, one can't help but see growth!

It is such fun to celebrate each other's special days, to pray for each other, to send or receive a surprise postcard of loving affirmation, and to be handed a small package to open later as you board a plane for some distant destination. The depth of benefit experienced from receiving and giving such support is tremendously meaningful and can only be measured in the heart.

The turning point in my marriage came when a group of women loved me enough to hold me accountable for my actions and choices. I was very angry with some of my husband's attitudes and actions. They asked me a sobering question, "Regardless of what Dave is doing, Jan, who have you become?

When I got honest and looked in the mirror of God's word, I saw someone who justified her tendency to be reactive by what she perceived to be her husband's arrogance. I lacked self-control and was not choosing to be responsible for my choices. I was a competitor with a closed mind. Without these courageous women in my life at that point in time, I would have continued with my "poor me," victim mentality. Usually the only place that attitude leads us is down the toilet. How grateful I am to my inner strength team. They challenged me into maturity.

The redwoods in Northern California are beautiful, majestic trees that grow 150–200 feet high, yet they have an incredibly shallow root system. When I discovered this about the redwood tree I was instantly curious. How do they withstand the fierce winds that blow off the Pacific Ocean? They grow in groves. The roots of one redwood tree reaches out and intertwines with the roots of another redwood which in turn reaches out to other redwoods. It is rare to see any large redwood tree standing alone.

Similarly, when crises hit and the storms of life threaten to overwhelm us, we too can stand if our roots are intertwined with the roots of others in the Body of Christ. The time to prepare for our challenging times is now. Develop an inner strength team.

You've no doubt heard the story of the woman who was about to jump off a high bridge and commit suicide. Another woman came along and the two of them sat down to talk. After an hour, both of them jumped off the bridge. None of us can survive indefinitely if all the voices coming our way are degrading, negative, and judgmental. Make a specific prayer request that the Lord will give you a cheering section and will allow you to be the cheering section for someone else.

ACTION STEP

In your journal list the women you consider to be part of your inner strength team. Send each of them an e-mail or note to let them know how precious they are to you. Pray for them.

Is there a specific way they can assist you? What do you need from them? What do they need from you?

If you don't have an inner strength team at this time, ask God to help you develop one. Reach out, in one concrete way, to someone who could use your support today. Become a certified card carrier in the royal company of the stretcher-bearers. Reach out in love to your neighbors: be a healing agent where people hurt, be a catalyst for change to right wrongs; be a prophetic voice to speak God's Word for the hour.

STEP #3

Face My Past (Part 1)

Today you are about to discover what you believe about yourself at the absolute core of your being. Is it an accurate truth or is it full of misbeliefs caused by a history of fear, pain, and confusion? Eleanor Roosevelt is quoted as saying, "Somehow we learn who we really are and then live with that decision." Today you get to examine the unquestioned or unexamined identity that you have accepted as true about yourself.

GET REAL ABOUT YOUR PAST

What do you remember about your life between the ages of birth to five years? Six years to 10? Eleven years to 14? Fifteen years to 20? Take the time to get comfortable and to really let your mind wander into your past. Perhaps you will find it helpful to play some soft music, to close your eyes and be still. Ask your heavenly Father to take this journey backwards with you and ask the Holy Spirit to bring memories to your mind to aid you in understanding why you feel the way you do about yourself. Take plenty of time remembering experiences that will help you answer the questions below.

Remembering Family Relationships

Do you remember much about your parents? How would you describe your mother? Your father? How would you describe your relationship with your parents?

How would you describe your siblings? What kind of a relationship did you have with your sisters or brothers?

What about you upset your parents and how did they express their frustration to you? How did they describe you? What feelings did you pick up from them about the way you looked or about your academic accomplishments?

How were you compared to your brothers and sisters?

Were your feelings accepted and considered by your parents or did you grow up learning to distrust your own feelings?

Your Parents and Their God

Did your father have a personal relationship with Jesus Christ? How would you describe this relationship? How do you think your father viewed God? Did your father ever discuss his faith with you? What was your emotional reaction to these discussions?

Did your mother have a personal relationship with Jesus Christ? How would you describe this relationship? How do you think your mother viewed God? Did your mother ever discuss her faith with you? What was your emotional reaction to these discussions?

Your Parents' Relationships

How did your family view relationships with other people?

Would you say your family put a greater emphasis on relationships or accomplishments?

Did you feel valued by your parents?

Did you feel your parents valued each other? Did your parents enjoy or simply tolerate each other?

What was your mother's style of relating to others—dependent, independent or interdependent?

What was your father's style of relating to others—dependent, independent or interdependent?

What beliefs did you pick up from them about conflict resolution, submission, the importance of each person having goals and dreams, and the importance of their relationship with each other?

Your Parents and You

What did you have to do to win your parents' approval? How did they express their approval and disapproval of you?

Did you feel emotionally connected to both of your parents? Which parent do you feel closer to?

Are you similar to your mother? In what ways are you similar to your father? How are you different from your mother?

How are you different from your father?

What do you appreciate most about your mother? What do you appreciate most about your father?

How did your parents handle your developing sexuality?

How did they deal with your steps toward independence? What was their attitude about your leaving the nest?

Are your formative years a joyful experience to remember? In what ways have these questions stirred up emotions of sadness, despair, bitterness, anger, or even hate?

IS THIS ABOUT BLAME?

No. Blame depletes energy, consumes us and keeps us prisoners of the person we blame. Blame keeps us stuck. This is about accountability. As Christian women, we are to honor what was honorable in our upbringing and to call a spade a spade when it comes to what wasn't honorable.

Even though we are not solely a product of our past, a necessary first step in becoming interdependent is to examine whether our words and self-talk come from hearsay, from parents and peers, or from reality as we perceive it.

We act not so much on the basis of reality as on the basis of our perception of reality. I may see an attractive middle-aged woman approach me on the street. You also see her, and based on the warm, accepting relationships you have experienced in your past with women of this age group, you eagerly anticipate meeting this stranger. On the other hand, if I have felt rejection from my mother, from my aunt or from a middle-aged teacher in my past, I might be extraordinarily leery of coming face-to-face with her. The past affects our perception of the present.

As a child we learn who we are and who we are not from the people around us. This doesn't change as we mature. A teenager's peer group is extremely important to their search for identity. As adults we choose the people we have around us, and what we believe they think of us is crucial to our feelings and understanding of ourselves.

Where did that negative perception about yourself originate? When did your negative self-talk originate? Where did your fear of leaving the familiar, your lack of direction, and your frustration with your limitations come from? Facing discontent is necessary to heal the wounds caused by harmful childhood experiences.

The purpose of this exercise is not to tear our parents apart limb by limb. They also operated with limited emotional, spiritual, and financial resources at that time because of the realities they faced. The purpose of taking the time to remember is to discover where our positive and negative ideas about ourselves have come from. Perhaps we will also unearth how our concept of God has evolved, since many of us have difficulty understanding God as Father because of painful relationships we have experienced with our earthly fathers. Lastly, this journey backwards gives new insights into the relationship or lack of relationship our parents shared. Many of us, even today, are affected by that relationship which seemed so very normal to us for so long.

WHY BOTHER?

Do you question the necessity of facing the past? Is it painful? The first major reason why healing our memories is important is because we aren't free to love others in our present when we carry so many scars from the *past.* How often do we run into people who remind us of people who have hurt us in the past?

The second marvelous reason for facing the past involves the emotional release of facing and forgiving. Scripture promises that the truth will set us free. Let me go on record, however, as saying that at first the truth can make us sad, hurt, and depressed. When we face the truth, confess it, and forgive it, we are set free. For years many of us have barricaded a part of ourselves and have refused to let God's love reach inside. That unconfessed part keeps us in bondage. What freedom comes when we move towards the pain that we have been afraid to examine! We find a loving Savior who accompanies us on our journey, helps us to forgive, and will "hurl our iniquities into the depths of the sea" (Micah 7:19).

A third amazing thing happens. When we forgive someone who

has hurt us deeply, that person seems to experience a new freedom. One can only imagine what would have happened in young Saul's life if Stephen hadn't uttered these words to the Lord as he was being stoned to death: "Lord, do not hold this sin against them" (Acts 7:60). This was, beyond a doubt, one of the tools the Holy Spirit used as He transformed young, intelligent, well-bred Saul into the apostle Paul. Am I blocking a freedom the Holy Spirit desires someone to have?

The Lord has made *our* forgiveness dependent on our willingness to forgive, even if no one has asked us, and this is the last reason we need to face our past. Mark 11:25–26 states it clearly: "And when you stand praying, if you hold anything against anyone, forgive him, so that your Father in heaven may forgive you your sins."

ACKNOWLEDGING THE WOUNDED CHILD

If you happen to attend a church that emphasizes your unworthiness, sin, and guilt, you may live in a state of constant condemnation. You may never have experienced the freedom Jesus wants for you. The burden of this condemnation may have been so phenomenally overwhelming that you decided to rebel and prove to the world that you *are* acceptable by being spunky, getting even, or withdrawing behind a mask and eventually behind closed doors. Perhaps you've become the clown or little miss spirituality. Maybe you've lowered your standards to prove you were acceptable. Perhaps you've rejected your parents' lifestyle and joined a peer group where you found acceptance. Perhaps you choose to be so busy you don't have to think about the issue at all. Perhaps you've retreated behind a box of chocolates in front of the television set.

What happens in our lives when criticism comes from the people we're trying so hard to impress? Each of us faces that. We *all* fail and have to face our failures. But each time you face a failure, is it proof-positive, to your hurt inner child, that you are incapable, unacceptable, and stupid? Is failure a helpful teacher in your life? As your self-image became severely malformed by the blows life dealt, did you start to reject even the positive pieces of information coming your way? Today, how do you respond to a compliment? Can you say "thank-you" and accept it or are you uncomfortable receiving affirmations?

If you are involved in a relationship, do you find yourself clinging for dear life, afraid that he too is going to find out the truth about you, criticize you, and abandon you? Do you find yourself smothering the life out of him? If you are in a position of power, do you criticize and condemn others before they can do it to you? Do you come unglued when an employee finds fault with some facet of your business? Where did this germ of self-hate, which has spread into a cancerous disease, come from? No doubt, it began in harsh criticism, comparison, labels and even abuse.

WON'T THE PAIN GO AWAY?

I can almost hear some of you, sharing Paul's writing from Philippians 3:13–14 with me: "But one thing I do: Forgetting what is behind and straining toward what is ahead, I press on toward the goal to win the prize for which God has called me heavenward in Christ Jesus." You are telling me to forget the past. Today is a new day. I believe that there is only one way to forget the past; we must deal with it. Face the past so you can file it under "forgiven and reprogrammed." If we are full of fear, hate, and prejudice, these will dictate our behavior. If we think we can just shove the past under the surface and walk away from it, one day we will find ourselves in a new situation or in front of a stranger who will trigger a memory button. For no understandable reason we might find ourselves intensely disliking the stranger or dealing with a surge of negative emotions. If we assume the ostrich stance with our head in the sand, ignoring the past, we limit the healing the Holy Spirit desires to bring. We must deal with the past so we can begin to love ourselves, our God, and our neighbors. Proverbs bears repeating, "As a [woman] thinketh in her heart so is [she]" (Psalm 23:7, KJV). Denis Waitley puts it this way:

> All individuals are born without a sense of self. We are like tape recorders without the key message—with some prerecorded facts and background music, but no central theme. We are like mirrors with no reflections. First through our senses, during infancy—then through language and observation—we tape record, build and photograph our video, audio and sensory cassettes of ourselves. This recorded self-concept or self-image—this

mental picture of self—when nourished and cultivated, is a primary field in which happiness and success grow and flourish. But this same mental self-concept, when undernourished or neglected, becomes a spawning pond for low achievement, defiant behavior, and unhappiness."[14]

ACTION STEP

Take out your journal. Write nonstop for 10 minutes any thoughts that come to your mind about any destructive words spoken to you which have deeply impacted your view of yourself. If you need a prompt, ask yourself, how did my family shape my self-esteem? What were the crossroad moments in my life, moments that changed how I saw myself?

"A lie unchallenged become the truth. Today make the choice whether your past determines your future."

JANET CONGO

STEP #4

Deal With My Past

Would you believe that a 10-ton elephant can be tied to the same size stake that a 300-pound baby elephant is tied to, yet never pull it out? This is true because of two facts. Elephants have great memories, and frankly they're not too smart. As a baby, the elephant was secured at this stake. Try as he might, he found it impossible to escape. For the rest of his life, even though he grew into a 10-ton elephant, the animal remembers he cannot get away and so he doesn't. He lets his past define his present.

Are we a little like that elephant? Did someone in our past tell us we weren't pretty, we wouldn't amount to much or we were stupid? When did we start believing them? When did we drive an elephant stake into our subconscious mind? As adult women, are we being held back by some erroneous stake from the past?

My sixth grade teacher, who also happened to be my first male instructor, told me (no doubt in desperation) in a physical education class one day that I was the clumsiest person he had ever seen. That comment hurt, and it has stuck with me all these years. To this day when I walk in front of a group, especially men, that stake wants to hold me down. I was also the adolescent with the purple acne. It cleared up long ago, but when a pimple appears now it is easy to overreact with those adolescent feelings. A dear friend who has lost a great deal of weight shared with me that she is working on reprogramming her inner tape because it is very easy for her still to feel tremendously overweight. What inaccurate tape is playing in your mind? What "elephant stakes" have you driven deep in your subconscious? Do you desire to be healed, to cooperate with our Lord by pulling the stakes out? Or do you want to continue the pattern you have established?

DEAL WITH YOUR PAST

If the ache is excruciating enough and the pain so intense that you desire the Holy Spirit's healing touch on your memories, consider five steps you can take to effectively deal with your past.

1. Invite the Holy Spirit to Take Part in Your Journey

This is not a journey for us to embark on alone. This is not a solo flight. For this voyage we need to depend on our Lord and on His Holy Spirit.

"Here I am! I stand at the door and knock. If anyone hears my voice and opens the door, I will go in and eat with [her], and [she] with me" (Revelation 3:20). God is available for our personal journey, but he wants us to extend the invitation. We must turn the tap on as it were. Imagine a broad pipe coming straight from heaven. This pipe carries all of God's grace, love, power and healing to each one of us. In the center of this pipe is a tap. What power we have! By turning the tap off we can shut off the flow of God to us. We can go thirsty if we choose to. Or we can turn the tap and open up the pipe so the power of God flows to each one of us. Our inner self is God's terrain, but we must take an active part in the exploration of that newfound land.

By choosing to be an ostrich, by refusing to face painful memories and hurts, we turn off the tap. We refuse to allow God's cooling waters of forgiveness and healing to touch our pain, and we will continue to find ourselves parched, cracked, dry and oh, so thirsty. I invite you to lay down your reading for a moment and invite the Holy Spirit to accompany you on your journey backwards. A written invitation is always a thrill to receive. Let's extend a written invitation to our precious Lord:

> Holy Spirit, today I invite You to walk down the corridors of my past with me. I ask You to bring to my mind incidents that have brought me pain, people I would just as soon forget because they have hurt me or I have hurt them. Bring to my conscious-

ness unhealthy attitudes and delusions I've been living under. Today I turn on the tap so You can flow freely to all of my pain and need. Thank You for coming, Holy Spirit. I don't want to stop the flow of Your Spirit ever again.

Signed,
(Name) ____________________
(Date) ____________________

Praise God! He is nearer to us than any problem, any conflict, any pain. Our Lord is in us and with us.

2. Listen to Yourself

What has your body been telling you lately? Our marvelously created bodies are in many ways alarm systems designed to go off when things are not right. Have you found yourself overwhelmingly fatigued for no apparent reason? Have you been furious and amazed at the depth of anger? What about depression? Do you find yourself depressed most of the time or do you only get depressed in certain situations? Are there roots of deep-seated negativity, jealousy, bitterness, and competition within you? What have you been dreaming about lately? Would you classify yourself as healthy or have you been physically ill a great deal in the past few months? When was the last time you had a physical? What is your body saying to you? If we are to love ourselves we must learn to listen to our bodies.

3. Face the Master Openly

When we accept Jesus as Lord and Savior, we give our lives to our Redeemer. With all His graciousness our Lord lovingly takes our gift and thanks us for it. We are sure we've given Jesus the gift of ourselves—but have we? Often what we've done is give the Lord the wrapping paper and the beautifully colored bow on our package. We give Him a superficial gift.

Jesus desires that we get to know ourselves deeply and give Him whatever is real—not just the shiny, pretty, sweet-smelling, competent parts. Clutter, garbage, and pain also fill our lives. Perhaps we have a prick of conscience periodically, but that prick fades as the years pass. Then we invite this Light of the World to be our Lord and suddenly all the garbage, clutter, and pain that has been festering is exposed. Jesus knows whatever is inside us—the hurt, pain, anger, fear. He is never shocked by it. He is never repulsed by it. Why, that's what He died for! He came to this earth to redeem it. But what do we do? Often we slam the door, pretend the pain isn't there, act as if everything is wonderful and assume the stance of an ostrich. Just like the ostrich, if it doesn't work well to put our head in the sand, we run faster than anyone else and get busier and busier. If we are hiding our hurting inner child from anyone, it certainly isn't God! Most likely we are hiding it from ourselves.

4. Drop Your Masks

Over and over again we are told to do what is right even if the feeling aren't there; if we act as if something is true, eventually the emotions will follow. Never would I deny the truth of this statement—but in the area of healing memories we must apply it carefully. Taken to its extreme, this advice can result in phoniness. We act spiritual while we develop an ulcer because of our internal gymnastics. God is deeply concerned about our relationship with ourselves. He wants those of us who are divided to be reconciled to Him *and* to ourselves. This is never accomplished by wearing a mask.

I love Paul's writings! Paul was free to share himself with people. He writes, "We do not want you to be uninformed, brothers, about the hardships we suffered in the province of Asia. We were under great pressure, far beyond our ability to endure, so that we despaired even of life" (2 Corinthians 1:8). Never does Paul set himself up as "Mr. Perfect" to help people. But sometimes we, as Christians, use even our faith as an excuse for failing to be honest with each other. Our logic goes something like this: "I'm a Christian now. I'm not supposed to be depressed or have an uncontrollable temper. I'm supposed to have overcome these things. I'd better not let others know what I'm really like or they won't think I'm much of a Christian." So we put on a mask and our pride gets entangled in the mask. We're phonies and we know it, but we must keep others from guessing the truth. The result is that we end up lonely and cut off from others. We think we are hiding our secrets, but really our secrets are hiding us. The longer we pretend, the stronger grows the gnawing fear that sometime we'll let the mask slip. The very act of secrecy makes us inaccessible to love.

We are in need of a Savior. After all, isn't that why we asked Jesus to be our Lord in the first place? It is only pride that tells us we must minister as the strong one to the weak. In reality we are called to minister as one needy human being to another needy human being. When we minister by acknowledging our own need, others come away seeing the magnificence of our Lord. They desire Him, they praise Him, and they see their need of Him rather than thinking, "I can't possibly be as good a Christian as she is." It's the difference between seeing grace in each other rather than fueling guilt and discouragement.

ACTION STEP

Pause right now and ask the Holy Spirit to make you aware of the masks you have been wearing. Spend some quiet time waiting on the Lord about this matter. As the masks and the phoniness come to your mind, confess and ask the Lord for His forgiveness. Confess that once again, you've tried to be the all-perfect one instead of letting God be the all knowing, all wise, holy, perfect, loving Father. Ask the Holy Spirit to make you aware the next time you start to hide behind another mask. Enjoy the healing as it comes straight from the hand of God. Be refreshed in Him! Praise and thank Him for His all encompassing forgiveness, acceptance and love.

5. Understand the Source of Your Pain

This chapter has been full of questions that I pray have been helpful to you in reviewing the stages of your past and unearthing memories that still cause you pain. As pain that has festered for years is exposed to the Light, we see three sources of pain. First, *perhaps we locked the doors in our life because of sin—something we have done or neglected to do.* Perhaps we haven't used the gifts the Lord has given us. Perhaps we have used our gifts only to build our kingdom, and the result has been pain.

Second, *pain may be caused by something that someone has done to us.* This pain, on a conscious or subconscious level, is the result of another's sin against us. I have a dear friend who had a recurring problem that revolved around an inability to trust men. As she sought the Holy Spirit's assistance in walking through her past, a picture flashed into her mind of an uncle sexually molesting her. Perhaps you were abused as a child or raped as an adult. You especially know the excruciating pain of having someone sin against you. Perhaps you have been the victim of withheld love. Others can cause us much pain, and if it hurts too much and we feel incapable of doing anything to stop their sin against us, we often shove that hurt under the surface and into our subconscious.

Lastly, *festering sores in our emotional lives may come from something that happened to someone else we care for deeply.* We pick up someone else's pain and carry it. But did you know that often the other person is not carrying the pain at all? To this day I find it easier to be criticized myself, which is not a lot of fun, than to hear my family criticized. Perhaps this is an area that we who have been or are pastors' wives are particularly susceptible. In our very first pastorate I had a lady turn to me during the Sunday morning worship service with these words, "Doesn't your husband have anything else to wear? I'm so tired of seeing him in that one suit." Believe me, this is a mild example of what happens to pastors' wives and children. But whatever the situation, perhaps you have been carrying someone else's pain all these years.

NOW LET CHRIST HEAL YOUR PAST

As women eager to invite the Holy Spirit to mold us into interdependent women, we must be willing to make crucial choices deal with our own past.

I Choose to be Dependent of God's Resources

Building the kingdom of "me" will not release the inner hurts and tapes of my past. My highest aim in life must be to know Christ. Often in this process we need to be willing to wait, the very thing many of us find most difficult. So many Scripture passages refer to waiting.

> "In repentance and rest is your salvation, in quietness and trust is your strength" (Isaiah 30:15).

> "But those who hope in the Lord will renew their strength. They will soar on wings like eagles; they will run and not grow weary, they will walk and not faint (Isaiah 40:31).

> "I am the vine; you are the branches. If a [woman] remains in me and I in [her], [she] will bear much fruit; apart from me you can do nothing" (John 15:5).

There is no shortcut to cooperating with God in changing ourselves. It involves waiting silently; it involves filling our minds with God's Word; it involves meditation.

When we try to love independently of God's resources we often do it to get something back, to manipulate, or to impress. Let's ask God for the love and compassion we need to love ourselves and others.

I Choose to Change My Pattern of Rehearsing Past Hurts

In the past, when we have experienced deep hurt, likely we responded in one of two ways. We either rehearsed the hurt so faithfully that we hated the person who hurt us, or we withdrew from the situation. Both responses are dangerous. In the first instance we end up being controlled by the person we are cursing. In the second we have erased the possibility of a positive message overriding the hurt. We have closed out both God's love and the human love that others want to give us. Let's change our pattern. Let's stop flogging others and flogging ourselves. Let's focus on God's forgiveness and acceptance of us. Let's stop waiting for some magical time when all of our unrealistic standards for ourselves and others have been met. Judas focused on his guilt and hung himself. Peter focused on our Lord's forgiveness and he hung up the guilt. Let's do likewise.

I Choose to Own My Pain and Acknowledge My Past

The longer I nurse my hurt or rehearse my guilt, the harder it is to let it go. Rarely am I the sole victim in my relationships; often I have had a part in adding to the pain I experience.

Many of us have a tough time moving away from our pain, owning our part and moving towards forgiveness. We refuse to take this step until we receive an apology or at least an acknowledgment of the validity of our hurt feelings. In an ideal world, we would get both immediately. In the real world holding on to blame and resentment hurts us far more than the original injury. It not only keeps us stuck in the past, but it also discolors our existing and future relationships, imbuing them with hostility and distrust.

I Choose to Forgive

I find a prayer journal an extremely helpful tool for writing out my personal prayers of confession. After them I often write the words of I John 1:9: "If we confess our sins, he is faithful and just and will forgive us our sins and purify us from all unrighteousness." I also find my journal useful when I need to work through the hurt someone else has caused me.

I choose to forgive. I do this because of my Lord's example. As I write this, Easter is one week away. I have been meditating on the day prior to and following Christ's death and resurrection. He poured His life and love into people's lives and they rejected Him. He was jeered and publicly humiliated. He was hung between two common criminals. Not one of the jeering mob sought His pardon at Calvary. What was His response? He asked for God's forgiveness for those who did not know what they were doing to the Son of God. His attitude bears no resemblance to my natural tendencies. I would want those people to suffer.

Peter once asked Christ how often he would need to forgive someone who had offended him. Jesus' reply was "as many as seven times seventy." On Calvary, the creator God of the universe lived out the truth of His words. We are often called to repeatedly forgive—especially after family gatherings held during the major holidays! I choose to forgive. I choose to obey. It's up to God to release my emotions. That doesn't often happen instantaneously. It takes time as I am willing to move towards forgiveness in the time I've been given.

Sometime my willingness to forgive increases when I feel empathy for the person who hurt me. I see this happen in the counseling office on a regular basis. Perhaps someone has been devastated by a parent's choices. When she researches that parent's background and begins to understand the deep wounds her parent carried, she sees how the sins of the grandparents or great grandparents have visited the second or third generation. Empathy for our parents' woundedness and understanding the forces that shaped our parents' lives can assist us in moving away from blame and toward forgiveness.

When we forgive someone who has hurt us, we do not necessarily reconcile. Trust is something that must be earned over time. Forgiveness is a choice I make for my own good. Corrie Ten Boom, once imprisoned in a concentration camp for helping Jews during World War II, has been quoted as saying, "To forgive is to set a prisoner free and to find out that prisoner is me."

I Choose to Celebrate the Personal Growth in Me

My prayer needs to be: *Lord, help me to learn positive lessons from the hurtful things I encounter in life*, rather than praying, *Lord, don't let me be hurt anymore*. In our world people who minister must have experienced pain and found God in the midst of it. These women will be less likely to throw out pat, thoughtless answers. They will be less likely to clobber you with Scripture verses. They will be less likely to resemble Job's comforters. They will listen, love, and lead you to the resources of the Lord Jesus Christ. They will be strong in their broken parts.

I Choose to Love Unconditionally and Creatively the Person Who Hurt Me

Jesus Christ offers us an unconditional, initiating love. How many times do we put "ifs" on our loving? We tell ourselves that if she will do such and such, *then* I will love her. God's love does not depend on what we do or what others do. Thank goodness! It's as if we have a giant magnifying glass within our heads; a glass that enlarges the negative in ourselves and others. Our love does not depend on other people meeting our expectations. Our love depends only on God. Then in faith we act.

Have you thought of asking God for His creativity in loving someone you've been struggling against? Have you asked God to help you see that precious person through His eyes? Sometimes it is necessary to mourn the relationship we hoped for but never had. After we have worked through that process, with the Holy Spirit's guidance, it is easier to go on with reality-based expectations for that person.

There is a person in my life whom I love, but whose relationship with me has been a personal disappointment. She is incapable of giving me the type of relationship I desire. She didn't live up to my expectations. In fact, I've had to grieve my expectations. This relationship has taught me many valuable lessons, including one on love: you learn to love by giving love even if the other person doesn't respond as you wish she would. In prayer one day the Holy Spirit convicted me that I needed to make it a point of doing one affirming thing for my friend each week, even while I was going through this mourning process. It's been fascinating to watch the relationship slowly, oh so slowly, take a turn for the better. As I choose to creatively love the person whose passivity has hurt me, I have discovered the Holy Spirit doing a loving work in me. The pain provided a doorway for personal growth. In my life I have had to acknowledge that the first step towards interdependence is a step backward.

ACTION STEP

Who do you need to forgive? Write down their names. Beside each person's name acknowledge where you are in this six-step process. Ask the Lord for His help in doing what it takes to move to the next step. If you find yourself stuck, perhaps you would benefit from working with a Christian counselor.

"Freedom is what you do with what's been done to you."

JEAN-PAUL SARTRE

"I love to the degree that I forgive."

JANET CONGO

STEP #5

Let God Heal My Past

Three teenagers boarded a bus in New Jersey. They couldn't help noticing one of the passengers, a quiet, poorly dressed man sitting alone and silent. When the bus made its many stops everyone but this man got off.

One of the teens gathered his courage and talked to the man. At the next bus stop everybody got off again except the man. The same teen invited the man to get off the bus and stretch his legs. He accepted the invitation.

One of the teens commented, "We are going to Florida for a week in the sun. We can't wait. We've never been there, have you ever been in Florida?"

"Oh yes," he said, "I used to live in Florida."

Curiosity took over and one teen asked, "Well, do you still have a home and family there?"

The gentleman hesitated. "I don't know," he finally answered. Caught up by the kids' warmth and sincerity, he shared his story with them: "Many years ago, I was sentenced to federal prison. I deserved to go there. I committed a crime. I had a beautiful wife and wonderful children. I told my wife not to write to me. I didn't write to her because I didn't want our children to know that their dad was in prison. I even told her to divorce me and find a man who would be good to her and the children. I don't know if she kept her part of the bargain; I kept mine.

He shifted awkwardly in his seat, afraid that he'd said too much. The eyes looking back at him were compassionate, so he continued. "Last week when I knew for certain that I was getting out of prison, I wrote a letter to our last address just outside of Jacksonville. I wrote, 'If you are still living there and get this letter, if you haven't found someone else and if there is a chance of you taking me back, here's how you can let me know. I will be on the bus as it comes through town. I want you to take a piece of white cloth and hang it on the old oak tree right outside of town.'"

All four of them got back on the bus quietly. When they were about ten miles from Jacksonville the three teens moved to the man's side of the bus and pressed their faces against the window.

Just as they came to the outskirts of Jacksonville, they saw an old oak tree. The teens let out a yell and jumped out of their seats. They hugged each other and danced in the center aisle yelling, "Look at it, look at it!" The entire tree was covered with dozens of pieces of white cloth. They could recognize a white bed sheet, a white dress, a little boy's white pants and white pillowcases.

I heard this marvelous story years ago. I have no idea of the source, but I do know how it impacted me. I was overcome with the awareness of amazing unmerited grace. This is the way God treats me if I will only believe it.

When I ask God to forgive me, He accepts me as holy and whole because of what Jesus did on Calvary.

> "I have swept away your offences like a cloud, your sins like the morning mist. Return to me, for I have redeemed you" (Isaiah 44:22).

> "As far as the east is from the west, so far has he removed our transgressions from us" (Psalm 103:12).

> "Their sins and lawless acts I will remember no more" (Hebrews 10:17).

Our God is never shocked. He knows the parts of us we aren't even aware of. While Satan is the one who condemns, Jesus Christ thankfully is not. He erases any record of my past in His memory. I am welcomed with no reservation back into His family. He declares my value in spite of my mistakes and failures. His redeeming work is the foundation of my self-image. Have you accepted God's gift yet?

A woman who was profoundly affected by God's view of her wrote these words.

> It's a woman's most treasured possession, a deep seated belief that she has worth—I longed to be anything other than poor and colored in a country that valued neither. I tried to convince myself that I had merit by being the smart girl, the nice girl, the one who earned people's attention and ultimately, their love. It took years before I understood that there was nothing I could look like, do, be, say, or think that would make me any more important in the eyes of my Creator.[15]

If you are having a tough time believing the truth that because of Jesus Christ's sacrifice your past has been redeemed, have a human voice reassure you. It could be a woman from your inner strength team, a pastor, or a Christian counselor. Accepting God's perspective as truth sets the stage to let your injuries go emotionally. In the face of trauma, we as human beings have the tendency to retraumatize ourselves. When we endlessly review, replay and rewind the trauma we etch it more concretely into our psyches. The only way to counteract that tendency is to accept God's validation of us, His recycling of our mistakes and hurts, and His willingness to give us a future.

So, on my journey towards interdependence the first thing I must do is reach towards the God of love, truth, power, holiness, forgiveness, and grace. He is unchangeable. He can't deny His own character. He can't get better. He is complete. He validates my worth.

Have you ever had the terrible reality hit you that someone you love no longer loves you? You are left helpless and powerless to change the mind of the other person. God is never going to do that to you or to me. His character is love. He will never betray His own character. He longs for you to walk in freedom.

I have found it helpful in my own life to hear a trusted friend speak Jesus' promise of forgiveness to me. We are just like Lazarus who when physically dead was raised to new life by Jesus' word. Even though he was alive, Lazarus' grave clothes had to be loosed by his close friends and family, who willingly took the grave clothes off of him and put up with the stench. In many ways we have been dead to a portion of our emotional self. We come to a new awareness of God's love, forgiveness, and acceptance through Jesus' Word. Then we must be released from all that binds us by the hands of a close loving friend or by the hands of a trained Christian psychologist or pastor willing to face the garbage, the hurt, the pain with us and point us again to a forgiving Lord. We often feel the reality of God's forgiveness more when spoken in audible terms by a human voice.

ACTION STEP

In your journal, write out the words of Isaiah 44:33, Psalm 103:12, and Hebrews 10:17. Personalize them by writing your name into them and then memorize the verses. Meditate on them.

Make a list of things you need to be forgiven for today. Ask God to remember these transgressions no more.

Write "forgiven and accepted" over the list.

"You are forgiven.
Your past no longer defines you.
Walk in the security of God's love."

STEP #6

Celebrate My Uniqueness

A Beverly hills plastic surgeon, Dr. Richard Fleming, told an ABC interviewer on the news show "Downtown" that he gets so many patients asking him to copy movie star's features that he compiles an annual list of favorite parts. For a steep price, you can buy Nicole Kidman's nose, Britney Spear's physique, and Halle Berry's cheeks. Too many women live to be a clone of someone else. It's as if we believe we reside in the wrong body. Life becomes a comparison game that leaves most of us wanting to be more than we already are.

Marlo Thomas has created a wonderful book entitled, *The Right Words at the Right Time*. In it she interviews people whose lives have been influenced by the right word at the right time.

Marlo tells how excited she was when she landed her first theatrical role. Soon after that she was devastated that all the interviewers only asked her questions about her father, Danny Thomas. As a result she went to her father and told him that she wanted to change her name even though she loved him very much.

There was a long silence and then Danny Thomas spoke. "I raised you to be a thoroughbred. When thoroughbreds run they wear blinders to keep their eyes focused straight ahead, with no distractions from the crowd of other horses. They just run their own race. That's what you have to do. Don't listen to anyone comparing you or me to anyone else."

While Marlo was preparing to go on stage the next evening, there was a knock on her door. She opened it. The stage manager handed her a white box tied with a big red bow. Inside was a pair of old horse blinders with a note that said, "Run your own race, baby!"[16]

When we begin with what we have, as opposed to what we don't have, we are often surprised at how very much God has given us with which to work.

ACTION STEP

1. Make a list of at least 10 things you like about yourself. Twenty things would be even better. No doubt the Lord has brought special people into your life who have helped you develop these characteristics and have affirmed your growth along the way. Put their names down beside your list.
2. Spend time in prayer. Thank God for the 20 things you like about yourself. Do you realize you are praising God for His creation when you do this? Then thank God for the wonderful, affirming people He has brought into your life. Finally, thank God for creating you.
3. Next, make a list of the things you honestly don't like about yourself. Go back and put a checkmark beside the things you *could* change if it were important to you. Please keep this list. We will refer to it later in the book.
   The unchecked items on your list are the things about yourself that you cannot change. The time has come to thank the Lord for these and to verbalize to Him your acceptance of these even if you view them as a "thorn in your flesh." Write out an acceptance prayer to the Lord. Choose to accept the limitations you cannot change.
4. Circle the words that apply to you from the following "I AM" list.

I AM

Ageless	Adventurous	Active	Beautiful
Balanced	Blessed	Charismatic	Creative
Capable	Dynamic	Determined	Divine
Enthusiastic	Eloquent	Excited	Extraordinary
Exuberant	Feisty	Faithful	Flexible
Free	Graceful	Genuine	Gutsy

Hardworking	Honest	Happy	Imaginative
Insightful	Individual	Influential	Joyful
Jovial	Kind	Kindred Spirit	Knowledgeable
Logical	Loving	Luminescent	Luscious
Magical	Motivated	Magnificent	Natural
Never Late	Noticeable	Optimistic	Observant
Perceptive	Poised	Persistent	Quick-on-my-feet
Quirky	Resilient	Reliable	Radiant
Sensational	Self-Assured	Spiritual	Trustworthy
Thoughtful	Unique	Unabashed	Understanding
Vibrant	Valuable	Versatile	Witty
Whimsical	Wise	Youthful	Zany Zealous
Zingy			

Our uniqueness is determined both by who we are and by who we are not, by our abilities as well as our limitations. Actress Sandra Bullock once said, "Your imperfections are what make you beautiful."[17] Let's not waste any more time asking, "What if?" or wishing we could be someone we aren't.

Joni Eareckson Tada has had to come to grips with the reality that she is a quadriplegic. That doesn't stop her from ministering in word and song, from being an artist, from writing or from encouraging others. Michelle Price came face-to-face with the reality of cancer and had to have a leg amputated. That hasn't stopped her from competing in winter sports events. As women, each of us will have to reinvent ourselves multiple times during our lifetime. Focus on the beauty of who you are, not on the person you weren't ever meant to be. Celebrate your uniqueness.

"There are only two ways to live your life.
One is as though nothing is a miracle.
The other is as though everything is a miracle."

ALBERT EINSTEIN[18]

"You are a living, breathing miracle."

JANET CONGO

STEP #7

Guard My Self-talk

"No one can make you feel inferior without your consent."

ELEANOR ROOSEVELT[19]

What do you tell yourself about your appearance, your talents, your physical and emotional well-being, your intelligence, your abilities, your value, your spirituality, and your work? What do you tell yourself when you make a mistake?

It seem to me that it's easier and more comfortable for many women to define themselves negatively than to own the wonder of who they truly are. The most powerful brainwasher in the world is ourselves. Your value is really solely up to you. When we talk negatively about ourselves we let our past seep into our present. We continue to rehearse the negative words that other people have spoken. If only there were a powerful antibiotic we could take to get rid of the thought viruses that infect many of us.

Proverbs 23:7 says that "as a [woman] thinketh in her heart, so is she" (KJV). So often our self-talk is negative, guilt inducing, competitive, fearful, anxious, and pessimistic. Our perceptions are like puppeteers who attempt to control our every move. Just as surely as a blacksmith hammers out and forges hot metal on an anvil, our thinking shapes our self-concept. We have pounded on our self with our internal perceptions and self-talk, and we have been pounded on and shaped by the behavior and messages of those we encounter in our life.[20]

Our internal dialogue and uncontested labels result in entrenched limiting beliefs. Three of the strongest limiting beliefs are that we are worthless, helpless, and hopeless. If we hold these beliefs as true, nothing anyone says, including Jesus Christ Himself, will change our personal truth. Once we own this negative perspective, we will shut out any conflicting information coming in our direction.

Michelangelo is often quoted as saying that inside every block of stone or marble dwells a beautiful statue. As a sculptor, his job was to remove the excess and to reveal the work of art within. As women who desire to walk in reality and truth, we must be sculptors too. We must chip away at anything that blocks the work of art in each of us. We must learn to listen to our thoughts, our attitudes, and our self-talk. If our internal dialogue doesn't agree with our Heavenly Father's view of us, we must challenge it. It is limiting and foolish to continue to use the judgments of others to define who we are today.

Our negative self-talk screams the loudest when our anxiety is heightened, when we find ourselves in a crisis or a confrontation, when we're risking something new, in an unfamiliar situation, or when we're in the presence of someone we admire. Tragic life events such as rejection, divorce, job loss, miscarriage, infertility, or an accident can leave us feeling inadequate and questioning whether we can measure up.

So often we treat our internal dialogue, our uncontested labels, and our limiting beliefs as fact. As a result we develop in-grown eyeballs that only focus on our defects. As we give attention to these faults, they seem to grow. One word of destructive self-criticism does about 10 times as much damage to your self-esteem as a word of criticism from someone else.[21] Women who consistently downgrade themselves will eventually come to the point of believing what they hear. Once they believe, they will automatically act on their beliefs.

It becomes obvious then, that our words program our spirit either for success or defeat. How do you talk to yourself? How do you talk about yourself? Do you build your own set of limitations by the words you say? Are your words faith or slave words? Does your vocabulary consist more of "I can," "I choose," "I will" or "I'm not," "I can't," and "I won't." One of the surest ways to lose our sense of self-worth is by persecuting ourselves with unreasonable, unscriptural, illogical, and negative thoughts.

If our thoughts and self-talk are so important, why do we bombard ourselves with negative self-talk?

Being negative has its payoffs—and we must learn to reject them. A person steeped in negativity often lives out the script of a martyr overflowing with self-pity or lives in such a way as if to prove she really is unlovable.

WHAT I GAIN THROUGH SELF-REJECTION

1. Self-rejection is an excuse for not accepting responsibility for my own happiness.
2. I can hide behind a smokescreen of inferiority rather than admitting that I don't know who I am. I only know who I am not.
3. I can avoid the risk of sharing my honest feelings.
4. I can be lazy about maximizing my growth.
5. I can hold on to a bag of self-condemnations in an effort to endear myself to others.
6. I have a perfect justification for continuing to be dependent on others rather than facing life on my own.
7. I have an excellent justification for failure.
8. I have a valuable reason for indulging in self-pity.
9. Satan's off my back. After all, I'm doing his work for him.

We make ourselves small or great depending on our thought life. Perhaps you have been blocked from valuing yourself because of a false understanding of humility. Do you believe that denying yourself is the same as demeaning yourself? Phillips Brooks, an Anglican minister and author of the Christmas carol, "O Little Town of Bethlehem," said: "The true way to be humble is not to stoop until you are smaller than yourself, but to stand at your real height against some higher nature that will show you what the real smallness of your greatness is."

The interdependent woman is the only woman who can stand tall and give life all she's got because her God is so much greater. She stands in awe of the love and beauty of God's plan. She is both truly humble and enthusiastically proud that she can have a part in touching a hurting world with God's love. The opposite of pride is not humility; it is shame. We must give ourselves the same respect, generosity, and kindness that we would give to anyone we love deeply. We are to love our neighbor as ourselves. The only grace that any of us ever has is the grace that we bestow on ourselves and then pass on to others. Living consciously means that I take responsibility for the words that come out of my mouth. Am I willing to live with the results that I create in myself if I continue to rehearse those thoughts and speak the words?

ACTION STEP

Carry your journal with you for an entire day. (Try a week if you dare!) Record your internal dialogue, your self-talk. What did you learn? Are there ways that you have been limiting yourself as a result of your self-talk?

How do you contribute to your own lack of self-esteem?

"Love for self is something only we can choose.
It must be nurtured on a moment by moment basis
because it is the foundation from which we love and care for others."

JANET CONGO

STEP #8

Identify My Detrimental Beliefs

No matter what we face in life, the meaning or value of that experience is determined by our perception of it. Some people when confronted with challenges panic and fall apart. Others rise to the challenge. What accounts for the difference? William Shakespeare provides the answer, "There is nothing either good or bad, but thinking makes it so."

Scripture put it this way: "As a [woman] thinketh in her heart, so is she" (Proverbs 27:3, KJV). Our thoughts and attitudes determine the emotional reaction we have to any event. Each of us determines the meaning and value of whatever we face in life.

Dr. Victor Frankl, an Austrian psychiatrist was captured by the Nazis during World War II. He was taken to Auschwitz, the hell hole of concentration camps. His beloved wife and parents were murdered. His life in every way seemed to be under enemy control, yet in that forsaken place he discovered one thing that the Nazis could not control. They could not control the meaning that he assigned to this torturous experience. Each of us, if we choose, can create value from the toughest experience life hands us.

The attitudes we harbor and the way we think impact our feelings. Our emotions are a direct result of the way we perceive our experiences. If we turned Proverbs 27:3 into an equation, it would look like this.

A B C	A≠C	A+B=C
Activating Event	+ Belief (Thinking)	=Consequences (Feelings)

Often we delude ourselves into believing that an event or a person causes our emotional reaction. This is false. We think our way into our feelings. If when I am laid off at work, I tell myself, "I am a born loser, I'll never get another job. This is the end of my career." My emotional reaction will be radically different than if I think, "This is so disappointing, but I really am never sure what is good news or bad news in my life. Perhaps this is an opportunity to explore some options I've only daydreamed about." We are the ones who make ourselves feel depressed, worried, or angry. If we accept this truth, we will understand that we can change our feelings by examining our thinking.

David D. Burns, M.D. has created a list of thinking patterns that are guaranteed to create an unhealthy feeling response. As you examine this list ask yourself whether you regularly think in these destructive ways.

DISTORTED THINKING

1. All or nothing thinking: You look at things in absolute, black-and-white categories.
2. Overgeneralization: You view a negative event as a never-ending pattern of defeat.
3. Mental Filter: You dwell on the negative and ignore the positive.
4. Discounting the Positives: You insist that your accomplishments or positive qualities don't count.
5. Jumping to Conclusions: You conclude things are bad without any definite evidence.
6. Mind reading: You assume that people are reacting negatively to you.
7. Fortune-telling: You predict that things will turn out badly.
8. Magnification or minimization: You blow things way out of proportion or you shrink their importance.
9. Emotional Reasoning: You reason from how you feel: "I feel like an idiot, so I must be one."
10. Should" statements: You criticize yourself or other people with "shoulds," "shouldn'ts," "musts," "oughts," and "have-tos."
11. Labeling: Instead of saying, "I made a mistake," you tell your-

self, "I'm the mistake, I'm a jerk or a loser."

12. Blame: You blame yourself for something you weren't entirely responsible for, or you blame other people and overlook ways that you have personally contributed to a problem.[22]

If we are creating our own misery by harboring any or all of these thoughts, we will find ourselves feeling hopeless, hurt, inferior, depressed, anxious, angry, and miserable. We will effectively zap most of the energy we need to creatively deal with whatever life hands us. If we have made it a habit to hold these distorted beliefs, then they will come automatically.

Journaling will become your lifeline when you have made these distortions a habit pattern. When you find yourself in an emotional funk, pull out your journal and follow these action steps.

1. Identify your distorted thinking. Check the list above. Write down the thoughts that are responsible for your emotional misery.
2. Ask yourself, "How will it help me or how will it hurt me if I continue to think this way?" Write down your response.
3. What evidence is there that your thought is true or not true? Record your response.
4. Would I say this (my distorted, negative thought) to a friend who faced a similar dilemma? If I did, what would be the result in my friend's life?
5. I am an imperfect, unfinished human being. Is there some truth that I need to face as a result of the predicament I find myself in? Keep writing.
6. How can I reword my distorted thought so that it is reality-based and positive? Get creative. Write down as many responses as possible. Encourage yourself as you would encourage a friend. For example:

   Distorted Thinking: "I'm such a screw up, a loser, a failure."

   Realistic Thought: "I'm human. I made a mistake. I forgot to turn an assignment in on time. I am embarrassed, but this certainly isn't the end of the world. No one has ever died of embarrassment. I can phone my boss, laugh at my absentmindedness and offer to drive the assignment to his home if it would be helpful. Humans make mistakes. Making a mistake doesn't make me a mistake. Next time I would be wise to put a reminder on my computer screen on the day before an assignment is due.

ACTION STEP

Think back over the past few days. What distorted thoughts did you allow yourself? How did you pay for that luxury emotionally? Replace it with a more realistic thought. When you read the realistic thought, what is your emotional reaction to it?

"Change your thoughts and you change your world."

NORMAN VINCENT PEALE[23]

STEP #9

Reframe My Story

Each of us is an ever-growing, changing and becoming individual. None of us is a finished product. There is no rigid picture of a Christian woman presented in the Scriptures; the women who followed Christ were free to be themselves. Mary and Martha had a special friendship with Jesus (Luke 10:38–42). Dorcas's gift of mercy was well known in her area (Acts 9:36) as was Mary's hospitality (Acts 12:12). Lydia was a successful businesswoman (Acts 16:14, 15), and Priscilla felt free to talk with Apollos about his erroneous teaching and correct him.

Nothing has to be static or fixed in our lives. Over our lifetime we may find ourselves pursuing one career or many. We may choose to stay at home and raise our children for a certain period of time. Life is composed of stages or seasons, and today you will no doubt find yourself in a different season than the one you were in 10 years ago.

The Proverbs 31 woman is an example of a woman using her gifts and abilities wisely and in season. She has been wrongly accused of being a Super Woman, an ideal that none of us can expect to attain—nor would want to. She has been misunderstood, and we have missed a source of strength if we have tossed out her model. Nowhere are we told that she accomplished all those feats in a day or even a year. She did it in her seasons and according to her needs and gifts and her energies.[26]

We are in process and we must be free to prayerfully define our own roles and careers as well as accept the differing decisions made by those around us.

Please don't let the role expectations that others have for you threaten your confidence in the roles you have prayerfully worked out for yourself. Your parents, in-laws, pastors, friends, and neighbors all may hold completely different ideas of what is "right" for you. Love those dear precious one and listen to their opinions. Then stick to what you believe unless the Lord shows you differently.

ACTION STEP

In your journal list all the different roles that you carry at this stage in your life. Thank God for the gifts and abilities that enable you to operate effectively in this season.

Not only do we choose different roles in different seasons, our life story has had many crossroad moments: moments that shaped us and were significant to how we feel about ourselves today. Each of has broken places in our story. Limits, losses, and mistakes temper our moments of seeming strength. The truth is that our real strength lies buried at the depths of any wound we have survived.

Instead of denying our disappointments, hiding our wounds, rehearsing them, or judging them, we need to accept them as part of our story. There's an old saying that captures this principle well; "You've got to be where you are to get where you are going."

Our wounds, disappointments, and losses can be like ice. When we resist them and run away from them, we keep on slipping into a place of pretense of defeat. Our wounds and our mistakes must be included in our life story, because they bring strength, insight, and courage to our story. As Christ followers, we believe Paul's words to the Philippian believers; "Being confident of this, that He who has begin a good work in you will carry it on to completion until the day of Christ Jesus" (Philippians 1:6).

When I received the crushing letter from the Department of Immigration that said I was not allowed to work in the United States, I felt as if my life as I knew it was coming to a crushing halt. With that proclamation our well laid plans collapsed. I couldn't teach. I loved teaching. Now what?

Little did I know or could I imagine that out of that nightmare would come an opportunity to begin writing. Out of the writing came the opportunity to teach at women's retreats, and out of that opportunity came the desire to work with women on a long-term basis in a counseling setting. That growing passion led me back to school to take another advanced degree. I doubt that I would ever have discovered either the passion to work with women or to work with married couples without this series of crossroads. Out of the disappointment came direction.

Don't run away from your mistakes or gloss over your mistakes. They are the source for so much of the texture in your life. That is where the learning happens. When you make a mistake, follow Benjamin Zander's example. He actively trains his students to lift their arms in the air, smile and say, "How fascinating!" When we screw up, the question is, What next?

We live, we make mistakes, we suffer, and we learn. Out of that pain, if we claim Philippians 1:6, growth, strength, and direction results. The greatest tragedy comes when we don't learn. Each of us must abandon the life of our dreams so as to embrace the life we are living.

ACTION STEP

In your journal record the different stages that your life has come through personally and professionally. Put them on a line graph. Make a separate list of all the abilities and gifts that have been developed in you as a result of the seasons you have experienced. Be sure to include the crossroad moments, and in those moments the wounds and mistakes that have added to your life texture and that have taught you so much.

"What the caterpillar calls the end of the world,
The Master calls a butterfly."

RICHARD BACH[25]

STEP #10

Evaluate My Tendencies

Now is the time to evaluate your personal tendencies in relationships. We each have the choice of dependence, independence, or interdependence with those in our lives. Many times it seems as if we swing the pendulum from one extreme to another depending on who we are relating to, or depending on the setting we find ourselves in. At work you may operate from an independent place while in your intimate relationship you may be more dependent. As you take the following questionnaire, focus on one relationship at a time. Then retake it with someone else in mind.

WHICH OF THESE DEPENDENT TENDENCIES DO I DEMONSTRATE IN MY RELATIONSHIPS?

1. Do I pretend to be someone I am not?
2. Do I pretend to like something that I don't in order not to offend?
3. Do I nod my head in agreement when I adamantly disagree?
4. Do I pretend to be more understanding that I really am?
5. Do I hesitate to express an opinion for fear that it would lead to conflict?
6. Do I find that my need to be liked is greater than my need to be honest?
7. Do I change my perspective or my style depending on who I am with?
8. Am I easily influenced?

9. Do I have a difficult time saying "no"?
10. Do I talk about myself in a demeaning way?
11. Am I inclined to put others on a pedestal?
12. Do I feel that solving another's problems or reliving his or her pain is extremely important—no matter what the emotional cost?
13. Do I find that the quality of my life is dependent on the people I am with?
14. Does my attitude depend on approval from this person?
15. Do I feel used, taken advantage of, resentful, and retaliatory much of the time?
16. Do I protect those close to me from the consequences of their behavior? Do I lie for them, cover up for them, and never say anything derogatory to them?
17. Do I assume I am in the wrong if there is any kind of conflict?
18. Do I believe my life would collapse if this person left?
19. Do I delight in similarity and conformity?
20. Do I have a difficult time making decisions?
21. Do I do anything to avoid this person's anger?
22. Have I shelved my own interests, needs, wants, and hobbies in favor of this person's?
23. Do I pretend that everything is fine when it is not?
24. Do I have a difficult time identifying and expressing my own feelings?
25. Do I want everything to be perfect and do I blame myself when anything goes wrong?

WHICH OF THESE INDEPENDENT TENDENCIES DO I DEMONSTRATE IN MY RELATIONSHIPS?

1. Do I get upset when I don't get my own way?
2. Do I get my needs met at any cost?
3. Do I find it difficult to listen?
4. Am I often exasperated by other people's lack of insight?
5. Am I adept at influencing other people's opinions?
6. Do I consider myself exceptionally perceptive at judging peo-

ple's character?

7. Do I speak my mind?
8. Do I own my feelings, thoughts, and dreams?
9. Do I suffer from a lack of patience?
10. Do I thrive on competition?
11. Do I feel angry if anyone or anything limits me?
12. Would I classify myself as a leader?
13. Do I tell people off?
14. Am I convinced that my beliefs are right?
15. Do I often feel like others don't do their part?
16. Do I feel angry a great deal of the time?
17. Do I blame others for my state of affairs?
18. Do I feel compelled to have the last word?
19. Do I use logic and Scripture to attack others or their positions?
20. Do I have a lack of patience for anything I perceive as weakness?
21. Do I have a difficult time asking for help or admitting need?
22. Is winning important to me?
23. Do I react defensively when questioned?
24. Do I rarely if ever let my guard down?
25. Do I have an unusual gift for knowing what is best for others?

WHICH OF THESE INTERDEPENDENT TENDENCIES DO I DEMONSTRATE IN MY RELATIONSHIPS?

1. Do I feel like I am a person who counts?
2. Do I tell the truth about what I like and don't like?
3. Do I own my emotions without blaming anyone else for them?
4. Do I accept myself as in process?
5. Do I accept others as in process?
6. Do I make time for myself?
7. Do I value and maintain friendships separate from my intimate relationship?
8. Do I refuse to be intimidating or intimidated?

9. Do I work through issues?
10. Do I know what my needs are?
11. Am I taking responsibility for meeting those needs?
12. Can I say "no"?
13. Do I set boundaries in order to protect love?
14. Do I communicate my truth by using "I" statements?
15. Do I encourage others?
16. Am I in touch with reality?
17. Have I worked on facing my past so that it is not interfering with my present?
18. Do I cultivate equal relationships?
19. Do I confront when necessary?
20. Do I respect myself and others?
21. Do I listen well?
22. Do I initiate acts of service?
23. Do I risk new ideas and growth?
24. Do I nurture my spiritual life?
25. Do I feel important and do I see others as important?

ACTION STEP

In your journal, record what you have learned about yourself as a result of answering these questions. Is there one area in which you would particularly like to see growth?

"To know what you prefer instead of humbly saying, Amen to what the world tells you, you ought to prefer, is to have kept your soul alive."

ROBERT LOUIS STEVENSON[26]

Control What is Controllable!

Two ingredients operate in every relationship. They are love and power. How these two are put together determines whether the relationship is healthy or unhealthy. Let me illustrate with the following continuum.

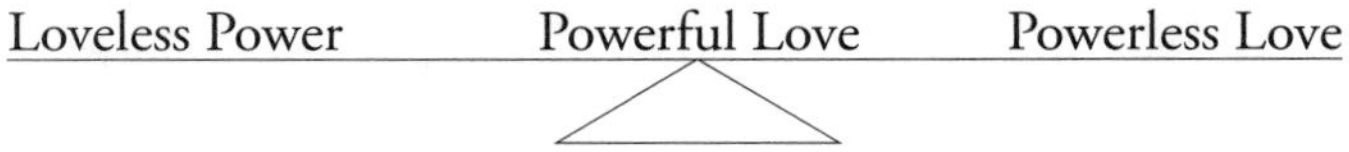

Susan was off balance in her relationships. She leaned towards the love end of the continuum. Her best friend Bridgette happened to be off balance toward the power end of the continuum. How was that demonstrated in their relationships?

Susan was loving, kind, thoughtful, and active in her relationship with Bridgette. Increasingly, though, Susan was feeling resentment. She felt walked on and taken for granted. Susan's bottom line in the face of conflict was "peace at any cost." Susan had stopped speaking her truth. She rarely said, "no." She didn't set any boundaries. She just gave in and gave up in the face of disagreement. In the face of any human irrationality she just surrendered her will and did not make waves. Her love was devoid of all power and so it became a powerless love.

Bridgette really liked her friend Susan, even though at times she found her passive, boring, and easily influenced. Bridgette liked having things go her way. In fact the few times that Susan dared to express a different perspective, Bridgette came down hard on Susan. She prodded and pushed until Susan finally acquiesced. Bridgette's philosophy was "my way or the highway," and because of it her relational style could be described as loveless power. It was all about Bridgette.

Both Susan and Bridgette, the dependent and the independent, were into control, but neither of them were controlling what was theirs to control. They were both attempting to control each other. Susan had the warped belief that if she was just "nice enough," Bridgette would always be a friend. Bridgette, on the other hand, controlled Susan to maintain her comfort zone. Both women had given up an extremely crucial kind of control—namely, self-control.

Jesus Christ is the only one who has ever put love and power together in a consistently balanced and healthy way. He was and is a powerful lover. His power was not only Holy Spirit-activated, His power was the power of self-control. Nowhere is that more evident than when He was hanging on the cross. He could have called ten thousand angels to overpower His enemies, but He didn't. He chose to stay on the cross and die because He loved. Christ never once used his power to dominate, to demean, or to take away anyone's freedom, choice, or voice. The powerful deity who spun the universe into being and who holds the galaxies in the palm of His hand emptied Himself of all loveless power. Yet the rejection of His dominance did not mean the denunciation of His power.

Jesus' words were, "You know that those who are regarded as rulers of the Gentiles lord it over them. … Not so with you. … For even the Son of Man did not come to be served, but to serve, and to give his life as a ransom for many" (Mark 10:42–45).

If Christ's attitude wasn't one of Loveless Power was it one of Powerless Love? No! Christ's love didn't avoid difficult issues or difficult people. He spoke the truth. He could say, "No." He spoke His truth whether conflict was the result or not. He was a clone of no one. The people in His life didn't mold Him into their image.

Christ's attitude was one of Powerful Love. His power made it possible for Him to walk with an angry mob, to refrain from accusing or attacking His enemies. He set His will like steel to be obedient to death. His love wasn't withdrawn when people rejected Him. Instead He continued to initiate love and truth, acts of service, and an attitude of friendship and forgiveness. In fact he said these amazing words to His disciples, "I no longer call you servants. … Instead, I have called you friends" (John 15:15).

Christ respected people. He communicated with them, laughed with them, celebrated with them, cried with them, prayed with them, sacrificed for them, and challenged them to grow. Little children felt comfortable with Him. He demonstrated profound tenderness and compassion while He embraced truth, freedom, and choice. Neither His love nor His power was selfishly motivated. In Philippians 2:5, Paul challenges us to "Let this mind be in you which was also in Christ Jesus." Nothing about this attitude is natural or easy. Only the Holy Spirit's control makes it possible to live out the attitude of Powerful Love.

If we understand Christ's attitude, then we acknowledge that we can't change, fix, or make other people do anything. They are free agents. Rather than reacting to, blaming, and feeling victimized by another's choices, we acknowledge that all we have control of is ourselves. The day that we become more deeply concerned about our own issues and attitudes is the day we free God's hands to work with us and the other person. We are each responsible for developing our own souls. No longer can our theme be, "I'll change if you change."

God is the only one who could justifiably control us and yet He refrains from doing so. He gives us freedom to choose. He weeps when our choices are destructive. He values freedom so much that He refuses to force us to do that which would really benefit us. Instead He invites us to love Him. That love transforms us from people bent on other control to people committed to personal maturity.

ACTION STEP

Answer these questions in your journal.

How am I most like Susan (living out Powerless Love) and how am I most like Bridgette (living out Loveless Power) in my relationships?

What would need to change for me to move toward the goal of Powerful Love?

Our goals, purposes and actions must be aligned in order to have healthy self-esteem.

"For God did not give us the spirit of timidity, but a spirit of power, of love, and of self discipline."

2 TIMOTHY 1:7

STEP #12

Examine Submission

The only woman who is free to submit is the interdependent woman. And when she uses the word "submission," she is referring to the concept of mutual submission in all her relationships, even her marriage. In her mind mutual submission is not involuntary subjection, a trade-off in domination, or self-negation. Neither is it a fifty-fifty relationship, in which she only contributes 50 percent and the other party does the same. Neither is it a relationship that allows one party to be used as a doormat.

Rather, mutual submission is the result of being filled with the Holy Spirit. Elaine Stedman defines it in a helpful way.

> Authentic submission is not reluctant nor grudging, nor is it the result of imposed authority. It is rather a chosen, deliberate, voluntary, love-initiated response to another's need. It is an act of worship to God, whom we serve in serving others. In no way, then, is authentic submission a violation of our humanity. It is appropriate to the purpose for which we were created, since in serving his creatures we are serving and worshiping our Creator. And it acknowledges the dignity of our humanity because it is service freely rendered from a will surrendered to the loving purpose of God.[27]

Submission is voluntary—a personal choice—and is only possible when we have a strong understanding of who we are. Mutual submission is only possible between two people who are aware of their equality before God and each other. The need for mutual submission is clear; it is impossible to share our faith in Jesus Christ by word and by example with someone we are treating as a doormat or with someone we have placed on a pedestal.

Mutual submission results from our awareness that in serving others, we really serve and worship God. It is possible only when we believe the command, "Be perfect [whole, complete, fulfilled], therefore, even as your heavenly Father is perfect" (Matthew 5:48) was given to both men and women. Therefore both members in the relationship will do their best to develop and affirm each other's gifts, talents, wholeness, and completeness. They are also willing to improve their communication skills—the ultimate tool of mutual submission.

It is not my purpose in this book to delve into the biblical and historical arguments about submission. If you desire a thorough study from a biblical perspective, may I recommend the books, *Heirs Together* by Patricia Gundry (Zondervan Publishing House) and *Gender and Grace* by Mary Stewart Van Leeuwen (InterVarsity Press). My purpose is to show how dependent and independent women misunderstand and misuse God's plan of submission. And, although this chapter carefully analyzes submission in the marital relationship, the information can be applied to our friendships and family relationships.

THE DEPENDENT WOMAN

The dependent woman has lost her sense of wholeness. She specializes in addictive relationships as a result. Her only sense of identity, apart from her relationships, is negative and inferior. Therefore she defines herself in relation to others, depending on them to determine her sense of self. She is the little girl always trying to earn someone's approval and pushing for uniformity in her relationships because that makes her feel secure.

The dependent woman is all too happy to turn over the controls of her life to a man—or so it seems. Since throughout her dating years she repressed her true self, she is all too eager to submit to the man in a marital relationship, becoming what he wants her to be and repressing her true self. That way she doesn't have to think and wrestle with issues.

In his book *How to Become Super-Spiritual or Kill Yourself Trying* John Sterner describes a woman who has opted for dependency:

> Suzy Submissive is totally dedicated to the care and feeding of her husband's ego. Each day of Suzy's life is filled with plans: She plans food that Fred will enjoy, sex that will excite him, and conversation that will be stimulating to him. She plans a fulfilling life for Fred.
>
> Suzy read somewhere that wives are supposed to submit to their husbands (Ephesians 6) and she has been doing it every since. The trouble is, Suzy is rapidly losing her personality, her friends and her cool. Her conversation is loaded with "Fred says" and "Fred thinks." Suzy has stopped thinking. She has also stopped going to church because Fred thought she was becoming too religious. She watches only the TV programs Fred likes and she has stopped seeing any friends Fred does not care for. She has for all practical purposes stopped living.[28]

Does submission mean destroying our individuality and never rocking the boat? The dependent woman believes that is exactly what it means. After all, this is how she lives.

May I introduce you to three dependent women who believe they are submissive?

June met and married her husband while she was in her late teens. She put him through school by working in a department store—a job she continued to hold until he became fairly established in a new business. She then stopped working altogether due to an insistent and persuasive Bible teacher who was certain the woman's place was in the home. Eventually two little children came along, and now at the age of 45 June doesn't know who she is or what she wants out of life. All she knows is this: she wants more than she's got. Absolutely nothing makes her content, even though she keeps quite a frantic schedule teaching home Bible studies.

June's reactions to her life are drastic and debilitating. The loneliness caused by her ever-absent husband is wearing on June, and she feels unappreciated and unloved most of the time. Her husband has not lived up to her expectations, and she is deeply depressed. In fact, she is spending more and more time in bed due to one "illness" or another. Her house is in a shambles and she is developing an ulcer from all the inner turmoil and anger she feels. On top of all this she has a gnawing fear in her heart that her husband is going to leave her. This thought almost suffocates her so she clings tighter and tighter to her man—even though the life she clings to makes her miserable.

Monica is single and hates every second of it. All her life her mother has told her she is nothing without a man, and Monica has swallowed her mother's philosophy hook, line, and sinker. Monica believes in her heart of hearts that men are superior, so she doesn't live her own life. Instead she gives her life to any available man, always hoping this will be the one to complete her. Since she doesn't enjoy her own company nor trust her own judgments or intellect, she latches onto someone who will provide the goals, rules, and orders for her life. She spends her life being someone else's person, with no self-identity. Needless to say, Monica is miserable. Because she considers herself to be only half a person she is continually attracted to men who are only half-men. Her latest romance was with a traveling salesman who she later learned was married.

Carol is a beautiful woman who also happens to be a talented musician. Carol was headed toward a master's degree in music when she first met her future husband, Dave. He was threatened by her gifts and she responded by erasing *her* academic goals and nurturing *his* dream—to become a pastor. The concept of oneness has always appealed to Carol. She believed she not only took her husband's name but also his identity. In Carol's case this means being a pastor's wife!

If Carol is honest, a part of her has never really wanted to grow up. When she first met Dave she was looking for a man who would care for her. She still wants this today. In her own words, "I need a man to lean on, to tell me I'm okay." Rather than accepting God's approval as well as searching internally for her own approval, she needs her husband's affirmation to prove her self-worth. Being a busy, preoccupied and often-threatened pastor, Dave has little affirmation to give. Nevertheless Carol waits like a small child for his nod of approval.

Carol is increasingly afraid to stand up for what she believes because her husband might be threatened and she might become unacceptable in his eyes. Out of this fear she refuses to communicate her truth in love. In fact she's often not even sure what her truth is. She is so terrified of rejection she can't say "no" to anything her husband wants and is at his beck and call 24 hours a day. She consoles herself by saying, "It could be worse. I could be single."

THE PAYOFFS

June, Monica, and Carol are dependent in their relationships with the men in their lives. But dependency has payoffs, and don't let anyone tell you it doesn't. First, the dependent woman feels cared for and safe. She doesn't have to grow up. Since she is familiar with what it means to be taken care of by parents, she is quite content to let a man take care of her, too.

Second, it is possible for her to feel more spiritual when she uses self-blame and self-punishment. This is the height of arrogance, because Jesus Christ has already bled and died as a sacrifice for our sin. The dependent woman somehow believes she can add to Christ's sacrifice.

Staying dependent requires laziness, and this is the third payoff for dependent women. Satan will either persuade you you're fine as you are or you're so very rotten you can't possibly change. It is then easier and safer for the dependent woman to stay stuck. The hard work of setting goals to change attitudes, thoughts, feelings, and actions can be avoided. This woman is certainly no threat to Satan!

As long as these women are able to blame others, they don't have to change. They will also get a great deal of sympathy from people who are also dependent victims. The dependent woman chooses to live in a personal fantasyland, never *really* desiring to change.

Women who believe that dependency and submission are one and the same have often been taught this style of submission from a pastor. Therefore they believe dependence to be the Lord's pattern for their life.

THE DEPENDENT WOMAN'S LETHAL WEAPONS OF CONTROL

But here is a trap and how easy it is to fall into it. A woman can pretend submission. How often have you heard a woman say something like, "He may be the head of this home, but I'm the neck that moves the head?" These women affirm their husbands by saying, "Whatever he says is right; after all he is the leader." But how often they dishonor their husband and themselves through their actions.

The dependent woman's lethal weapons of control are manipulation and retaliation. Notice the small step separating *being controlled* from *being controlling.* These women are the pussycat manipulators who resent their own lack of control so much they get back at their men—any way they can.

One manipulative method involves suffocating their men with kindness by babying them. By refusing to be honest about any issue or conflict, the dependent woman protects her man from self-understanding. She picks out everything from his suit to his deodorant, and how she delights in making excuses for him. The children, for example, are not to bother their father with their problems because he is exhausted and works much too hard. She babies him because she is terrified of change. She can avoid change avoided if he remains the same.

She can be dishonest with her words and actions. While claiming to be submissive and a follower, she can destroy her husband's financial base by wasting their money with unwise purchases. She can talk disparagingly to him by reminding him of every irresponsibility—every way he hasn't shaped up to her expectations. She can also choose to be disrespectful and divisive—like the pastor's wife I knew as a child who refused to go anywhere her husband was preaching. She can subtly shame him, use sex to manipulate him, silence to frustrate him, guilt trips to condemn him, self-pity and nagging to overwhelm him, and a poor state of health to blackmail him. She often waits until her man gives an opinion before subtly opposing him.

These women are dependent on their men, but their need for men is unhealthy. They seek personal security in their men but indulge, flatter, and attempt to buy them any way they can. In other words, they become masters of manipulation. It almost happens in self-defense, for no woman or man can experience emotional health when sense of self is defined by someone else.

THE INDEPENDENT WOMAN

This is the woman who reacts with horror to the concept of submission. Horrified by the misuse of submission, she "throws out the baby with the bath water" and isolates herself. She needs no one.

Although the dependent woman receives some payoffs from manipulating her partner within a submissive relationship, the independent woman experiences a temporary payoff by rejecting submission altogether. She feels in touch with herself and believes she is in control of her life by accepting relationships on her own terms and doing things her way. She becomes "anti-dependent." She ignores 1 Corinthians 11:11, which says, "In the Lord, however, the woman is not independent of man, nor is man independent of woman."

A middle-aged woman shared with me how she had decided to nurture her career rather than intimate relationships. She sold out to the business establishment and rose quickly up the corporate ladder—at the expense of healthy intimacy, however. Two relationships had been important to her, but not so precious that she would make concessions for them after her decision to make business her life. Eventually her personal relationships faded away. There she sat, beautifully groomed and financially comfortable but absolutely alone. She certainly had offers, but only, it seemed to her, from people who wanted to use her for their pleasure or to further their career. She was absolutely miserable. Ultimately total independence has no payoffs.

THE INTERDEPENDENT WOMAN

Relationship with the interdependent woman is not going to be as easy as a relationship with the "yes, whatever you want" dependent (Powerless Love) woman. It also won't be as competitive as a relationship with the "anti-dependent" independent (Loveless Power) woman. But it will be interesting.

The interdependent woman owns her own reality, emotions, ideas, beliefs, and values. She is also open to and interested in yours. She will not placate you, devalue you, or agree with you on every issue. Her life is meaningful and full. She is not in a relationship with a "significant other" to have him "take care of her." She marries because she loves, not because she is after fame, recognition, or wealth. Her life is satisfying and challenging. She chooses her relationships not to define her or complete her, but because this person would bring a richness, health, and fullness of his own into her life.

She doesn't need validation from a man to feel good about who she is. "Desperate" is not a term you would use to describe her. Yes, she enjoys men. She wants an intimate loving relationship with a man, but she doesn't define herself as a failure if she doesn't have one. She doesn't devote every waking moment to finding the man of her dreams. She deals in reality.

BENEFITS AND BLESSINGS

This type of relationship, as I have stressed before, will not always be easy, but the benefits will be overwhelming. I've included 17 blessings and benefits. Do you have any to add to the list?

1. It frees us up to be ourselves.

If we are married, our husbands fell in love with a spunky, interesting woman. Mutual submission gives us the freedom to be that woman for a lifetime. "It allows both husband and wife to contribute to the union from the richness of all that they are. It allows both mates to contribute all their abilities and attributes."[29]

2. We become real in each situation.

It forces us to get in touch with ourselves. Our feelings, thoughts, dreams, and questions suddenly take on a new importance.

3. We become much better listeners.

We genuinely care about other people's feelings, thoughts, dreams, and questions. This makes us a more effective communicator.

4. We acknowledge equal rights in a relationship.

David Augsburger and John Faul comprehensively define what this means:

> I am free to choose my words and acts;
> Therefore free to make mistakes.
>
> I am free to be spontaneous;

Therefore free to make mistakes.

I am free to trust my hunches;
Therefore free to be illogical.

I am free to be flexible;
Therefore free to change my mind.

I am free to live by my own supports;
Therefore free to refuse help and kindness.

I am free to take the consequences for my acts;
Therefore free to offer no justification for my choices.

I am free to love and care for others;
Therefore free to tell you without permission.

I am free to want relationships;
Therefore free to reach out for contact.[30]

5. We become affirmers to others just as our Lord is to us.

We learn to help other people believe that their dreams can become reality. Each person is helped to find, cherish and develop all that they are. Luke 6:31 puts it this way, "Do to others as you would have them do to you."

6. Mutual growth is a result.

As long as one person is not free to grow, the other partner won't achieve his full potential either. Both partners are helped to deepen, grow and change. "When husbands and wives live the way Jesus did, they do not play out roles in which one or the other hides away a part of himself or herself in order not to upset or displease the other. They trust God will be in their every move and then they move—even if it rocks the boat."[31]

7. We value each other equally as persons.

We acknowledge we are both equally important to God, to each other, and to the relationship. We mirror that belief through our actions.

8. Unity rather than conformity becomes an important value to each person.

Harmony is considered far healthier than being a revised standard version of someone else.

9. Each partner owns his own emotions, expressions, experiences, actions, and happiness or lack of it.

As a result we are not emotionally controlled by the other person or absorbed into the other person.

10. Both partners treat each other with equal respect.

They are "heirs together" of God's grace. Both people are valuable, therefore they will refuse to take advantage of each other or be possessive of each other. Feelings of intimacy and trust are heightened as a result.

11. We become equal in opportunity.

Both partners are free to be involved in ministries. Christ's world is in front of both, and He cheers us on while we cheer each other on.

12. Together we assume personal responsibility for the style of our marriage.

There is no longer a need to live by someone else's formula. Together we create our own style—our own "us."[32]

13. Our children become God's children.

They are entrusted into our keeping for only a short time. One person is not solely responsible for the raising of them. Neither is one partner cheated of the joy of really knowing his or her children as people.

14. We gain increased feelings of self-confidence.

This comes as a result of accepting our God-given identity and maturing as the Holy Spirit directs. We will no longer be dominated by others.

15. We will be increasingly dependent on the Lord Jesus Christ.

We refuse to be dependent on someone else for our spiritual growth and personal development.

16. Manipulation comes to a swift halt.

Instead, I give you the very best I have to give. I lift you up because we are equals. I serve you with joy because I love. We are free. Ponder these words by Nancy R. Smith:

> For every woman who is tired of acting weak when she knows she is strong, there is a man who is tired of appearing strong when he feels vulnerable;
>
> For every woman who is tired of acting dumb, there is a man who is burdened with the constant expectation of 'knowing everything;'
>
> For every woman who is tired of being called an 'emotional female,' there is a man who is denied the right to weep and to be gentle;
>
> For every woman who is called unfeminine when she competes, there is a man for whom competition is the only way to prove his masculinity;
>
> For every woman who is tired of being a sex object, there is a man who must worry about his potency;
>
> For every woman who feels 'tied down' by her children, there is a man who is denied the full pleasure of shared parenthood;
>
> For every woman who is denied meaningful employment or equal pay, there is a man who must bear full financial responsibility for another human being;
>
> For every woman who was not taught the intricacies of an automobile, there is a man who was not taught the satisfaction of cooking;
>
> For every woman who takes a step toward her own freedom, there is a man who finds the way to freedom has been made a little easier.[33]

17. Each partner takes responsibility for the home.

No longer is it only the wife's responsibility to keep house, hold an outside job, raise the children, and be a responsive mate. Therefore, she is freed from the necessity to be a superwoman. Rather, each partner takes personal responsibility for some of the mundane chores that need to be done in any home.

Dave and I find that Sunday evening, after our children have been put to bed, is a good time for us to make mutual submission a reality in our marriage. First, we share our individual calendars for the next week. We share our feelings about the week and the pressures that lie ahead of us. Next we examine each other's commitments and review our list of the mundane chores that need to be accomplished around our home. I know you face some of the same things each week in your home: laundry that needs to be done, floors that need to be vacuumed and scrubbed, and furniture that must be dusted—along with the grass and flowers that never take into account how busy you are! We divide up these necessities, making certain that there are a few items on our individual lists we enjoy doing. If your children are old enough, I suggest you include them during part of your planning time. It is their home, too.

We also find this a helpful time to check the goals we have created for ourselves, our marital relationship, our spiritual growth, and our children's development. This is the time to check up on how we feel we did during the last week. It's an opportunity to examine whether our goals are realistic and if they aren't, to re-evaluate them. Then we spend a precious time in prayer, committing each other and our week to the Lord and thanking the Lord for the gift of each other.

Lest you think that we have always done this, let me hasten to point out that this tradition in our marriage came out of total failure and frustration. At first this meeting time provided us with a way of coping with an unhealthy situation. It was in the process we discovered, with the Lord's leading, that we had stumbled onto something valuable. Feel free to use our idea or modify it to fit your personal situation.

ACTION STEP

In your journal complete these statements. Write a minimum of six sentence completions as quickly as possible without censoring them.

I am dependent when I …
I am independent when I …
In order to grow into interdependence I need to …

What did you learn about yourself?

"Where we stand is not as important as the direction in which we are going!"

OLIVER WENDELL HOLMES, JR.[34]

In what direction are you moving?

STEP #13

Face My People-Pleasing Tendencies

If you are traveling on an airplane with a young child, what are you supposed to do if the cabin loses air pressure and the oxygen masks drop from the panel above your head? That's right: as an adult you are to put your mask on first and then assist the child traveling with you.

Some of you may be thinking, isn't that selfish? Aren't we as Christian women commanded to take care of other's needs at the expense of our own? No! Consider the example from the airplane. If I chose to be selfless I could actually put the young child I was travelling with at serious risk. I would be unintentionally endangering the one I love by ignoring myself.

The superwoman spends every waking moment inflicting emotional cruelty on herself. She tries to keep everyone important to her happy at all times. She is left exhausted and depleted as a result of serving others while denying her own needs. She constantly compares herself to a fantasy. She compares everyone else's best with her worst. At the same time she pressures herself to be emotionally upbeat and happy regardless of the circumstances. Her underlying fear is that if she fails to do any of this perfectly, she will be punished, abandoned, or rejected by God and the people in her life. She can't live up to her own expectations. She feels like a total failure. She is depleted and demoralized. She is well on her way to being a totaled woman—a dependent woman.

Making ourselves martyrs is no way to make friends. Have you ever asked yourself why you go into the people-pleasing mode? Definitely the roots can go back to childhood or a confusion about the difference between self-interest and selfishness, but I believe there is another reason. When we are the one giving more to our family and friends, it may create a false security in our mind, a security that we are indispensable to these people. In actuality, when we don't let others give back to us in return, we are being manipulative and rejecting, whether intentionally or not. We are the ones who maintain the upper hand and the control in our relationships.

Inadvertently we diminish our friends. They may feel inadequate to reciprocate, embarrassed, obligated, uncomfortable, or even guilty. We rob those in our relationships of the great feeling of being able to give to us. We consistently over-function and teach the significant people in our life to under-function. We also turn ourselves into martyrs, always feeling that we carry the lion's share of responsibility in our relationships. Guess what? We do carry most of the load, and we are the ones who set that up.

Andrea Yates, a Texas mother of five children suffering from severe postpartum depression, drowned each of her children. She was given a life sentence. How I ached for her and for the absolute desperation she must have felt. One evening a friend e-mailed me a fabulous article written by a California school teacher, Dale Koscielny. It had appeared in newspapers across the country.

Confessions of a Changed Christian Mother

I do not blame Andrea Yates for believing that she was a bad mother and had no choice but to remove her "bad work" from the world. I understand because there was a time in my life that I believed, too, that I was a bad mother. My evaluation of myself and the products of my child-rearing, my four children, was not dissimilar from Yates'. As a 20-something, I married. I wanted nothing more than to please God and my husband, not necessarily in that order. We joined a small church: Jesus was preached, God was glorified. Pastor and wife modeled familial propriety and righteousness. And so, I did what Andrea Yates did. I left my profession, and rose to a higher calling: "Christian Mother." One baby came, then two, then three, then four. Blessed reward!

I kneaded and baked bread, soaked and simmered refried

beans, blended mayonnaise from oil and egg with just a dash of dried mustard. I purchased flats of half rotten strawberries and plucked stems, pared away soft spots, mashed, mixed, boiled and "put up" jar after jar of strawberry preserves, with my toddlers at my elbow. We, my husband and I, "in but not of" a materialistic world, covenanted before God to thrive on one income, to share one car. After children's bedtime, I sewed their T-shirts and shorts on my trusty Singer and embroidered pillowcases for each newly married couple at church. Not a very accomplished seamstress, what I lacked in skill I made up for in enthusiastic gift-giving. Ribbing on T-shirts could stretch over two heads; baby buntings resembled giant potholders. A close-out fabric sale netted six home-sewn brown and white plaid two-way stretch swimsuits.

In my "spare" time, I weeded dichondra, jogged the dog, hauled laundry to the laundromat and staggered under the weight of dozens of children's library books: Bible stories at breakfast, nursery rhymes on the potty, fairy tales at nap time. I know how clever Yates needed to be to keep all five babies clean and amused and enriched and refined; manners, of course, were learned at home. Housecleaning was a given. No nannies or Merry Maids for us. We are the Proverbs 31 ladies of the Bible, up before dawn, seeing to the ways of our household.

Instead of feeling fulfilled, following 15 years of never "getting it right," I felt frustrated: four shabbily dressed siblings bickered; tract-home paint peeled off fingerprinted walls; the car's head-liner drooped; and the dichondra lawn resembled a wasteland. I rebelled. I reincorporated four-letter words into my educated vocabulary.

I returned part-time to my profession. I scrimped to purchase a pre-owned Volkswagen Rabbit. I hired a cleaning lady, enrolled in ballet classes at the local college and resumed reading fiction. I had awakened to the impossibility of internalized expectations. I did not dump my faith, just switched churches. However, throughout my epiphany and my ensuing choices, I had the luxury of not being mentally ill, nor suffering postpartum depression. I was just very, very angry—at myself for trying

> to live out someone else's definition of a Christian mother, at my husband for being a bystander and at the church for not providing praise, offering grace or permitting diversity.
>
> I believe there is a part of Christianity, squeezed out from in between lines not written in the Bible, which plants the onus of family welfare on the wife-mother, minus the support system of the extended family available 50–100 years ago. Like Andrea Yates, I had the silent, self-incriminating definitions of Christian mother rushing around inside my head with no one to hear them, to refute them or to excuse me from insurmountable tasks daily set before me by my own unattainable standards. I do not blame Andrea, her husband Rusty or God. I am not sure who I blame. I just know that a woman's world can be impossible. We muddle on until we break away from our faith, or break up our marriage or just plain break. I pray for Andrea to receive medicines to stabilize her mind, for clarity in a renewed faith and for the forgiveness necessary to go on.

A mother who lived on a farm would go every day at noon into her kitchen, close the door, and make herself a cup of tea. She'd stay there for one half hour. She was not to be interrupted. Her little ones would bang on the door and ask her what she was doing. Every day her response was the same: "I'm making you a better mother."

What are you doing to fill your soul so that your giving comes from a grounded and centered place and not from a place of anxiety, burnout, and emptiness?

ACTION STEP

In your journal complete these statements. Write a minimum of six responses as quickly as possible without censoring them. What did you learn about yourself? I tend to overgive when …I fail to take my own needs seriously by …

Answer this question in your journal. Are there ways that I have been neglecting myself? (Spiritually, Healthwise, Exercise, Personal Appearance, Food Intake, Financially?)

If, as a result of your journaling, you discover that you have sacrificed your very soul in order to please, prioritize the ways that you have neglected you. Make one concrete step today your top priority item. You and those in your life will benefit if you are true to your own needs.

"Love your neighbor as yourself."

JESUS (MATTHEW 19:19)

"Unless I take care of my self, I won't be able to take care of those who matter the most to me."

JANET CONGO

STEP #14

Learn to Set Boundaries

When our daughter Amy was 10 years old she was devastated by a few girls who called her a bad name. Day after day she would come home from school in tears, hurt. I wanted to get across to her the concept of boundaries, but I wasn't exactly sure how to do that on a 10 year old's level.

One day I sat down with her and asked her to imagine that she was encased in a giant bubble. The surface of the bubble was hard as nails. When people spoke to her, their words were like arrows shot from a bow and arrow. When the verbal arrows came her way, they would hit the hard surface of the bubble and go "boing." At that point she had to decide whether those words agreed with what the Bible said about her value or if they didn't. If her classmates' words contradicted the high value with which God esteems each one of us, she was to keep her bubble hard as nails. After the arrow went "boing," it would fall to the ground. Oh yes, Amy would have heard those hurtful words and they would have stung, but she wouldn't take them into her heart and let them define her.

By contrast, if the word arrows shot in her direction were affirming of her worth and value, she could soften the walls of the bubble and let the words come into her heart.

Amy listened and then sat quietly. Finally she said, "I've got it. My friends who are always friends are like honey bees because they're sweet all the time. The ones who call me names are like bumble bees because I never know when they're going to sting me." She continued, "If I'm going to be healthy, I have to be a boingle bee." With that we both laughed. For about six months I'd walk into a room where Amy was playing with friends and every once in awhile I'd hear her say, "Boing." We'd look at each other and smile. She'd caught the concept of boundaries even if on an elementary level.

Boundaries are not about fixing, changing, or punishing another person. When I have healthy boundaries I take responsibility for what is mine. Boundaries are about self-control, not other control.

In healthy relationships, both people have a clear understanding of the treasures within their boundaries. Each of us before the Lord is responsible for our own feelings, attitudes, behaviors, choices, limits, desires, thoughts, values, talents, love, and words. I must take personal ownership of what is mine.

When we neglect or deny what we are responsible for, blame shifts and problem solving becomes an impossibility. Even if someone does this to us, we are still responsible to ask, What is my blind spot? What is my part in this problem? We must focus on cultivating the plants in our own garden rather than trying to control how someone else grows their flowers. We must adjust to what God and reality require of us even if our friend is not living that way. When there is a problem in our relationship, fault is irrelevant. We need to work towards resolution. (Matthew 5:23–24). When we have this attitude and when we put boundaries on ourselves so that we deny ourselves the freedom to say or do whatever we'd like in order to protect love, our relationship wins.

Only when we honor our separateness and own our boundaries, are we free to choose to love. Boundaries make it possible for us to love.

ACTION STEP

In my relationships, how do I take responsibility for the eleven treasures that are mine? Record your answer in your journal.

"We don't become mature by marrying into it.
Maturity is the direct result of taking responsibility for what is mine."

JANET CONGO

STEP #15

Speak My Truth

Early in our marriage, when I was mesmerized by the newness, I focused on our areas of agreement. I emphasized togetherness. My urge to merge resulted in my submerging my voice and swallowing my truth. In the process I became Dave's revised standard version. That was not altogether satisfying for me.

Dave says that if I'd just continued in that vein, we could have lived happily ever after. (He grins when he says that.) After a few years of swallowing my personal truth, I got very angry. Why wasn't my brain and my perspective welcome in our relationship? When I got furious I began living reactively. I'd give Dave more than a piece of my mind. I'd pat myself on the back for speaking my truth. However, I wasn't. By living reactively and speaking sarcastically, I was protecting both Dave and myself from the truth, from the conversation going deeper, and from a journey into intimacy. I had to face the truth that angry reactivity, criticism and self-righteousness was not the same as authenticity. Whenever the voicing of my truth diminished who Dave was as a person, I also was diminished.

There is an enormous difference between non-productive fighting and taking a firm position on our own behalf. When we fail to speak our truth, we assume a "de-selfed" position in our important relationships. We chose relationship at the expense of having a self. Usually at that point we act out our frustration rather than speaking it. When we quiet our voice and bury our perspective, we make ourselves vulnerable to depression, anxiety, headaches, chronic anger, and bitterness.

Sometimes we settle, give in and give up, fall silent and lose our awareness. Our wants, beliefs, priorities, and values become negotiable under relationship pressure. We create a pseudo-self, become an impersonator, zapped of energy, miserable and alone, disconnected from ourselves and others.

> Our conversations invent us. Through our speech and our silence, we become smaller or larger selves. Through our speech and silence, we diminish or enhance the other person, and we narrow or expand the possibilities between us. How we use our voice determines the quality of our relationships, who we are in the world, and what the world can or might become.[35]

Intimacy is only a fantasy if both people in the relationship are unable to speak their truth. Intimacy suffers in the face of silence and pretending. We can't be more honest with another person than we are with ourselves. It is not wasted time to get acquainted with yourself and your truth.

One of the challenges of intimacy happens when we find ourselves in the midst of an extremely uncomfortable interchange with someone we love. At that point we get to choose the self that shows up. When we're drowning in our emotions, we may think that we're thinking; the truth may be that we're only reacting. We need to be thoughtful and well prepared when we speak our truth.

Take a "Time Out" (explained in further detail in Step 18) if you are overly emotional, anxious, or defensive. Journal until you can see the big picture (we want to foster mutually empowering connections) and until you operate from your core values (how will my words affect the other person?) rather than in reaction to another's immaturity. Creativity asks questions and seeks to understand, truly understand, the other's perspective.

Speaking our truth requires practice. Each of us needs to learn how to define our perspective and how to stay connected when we don't get the response we'd hoped for. We must remind ourselves that no matter how effectively we speak our truth, we may not get the results that we want to get. At times it is more important for us to hear the sound of our own voice speaking our truth than it is to have the other person abandon their perspective. When we speak our truth we honor both our need for language and for self-definition.

At times speaking our truth may mean that we choose to model the behavior we want from others even if they aren't giving that to us. In many situations wisdom lies in being strategic rather than spontaneous.[36] It is important to act and speak for ourselves rather than against our significant other.

It isn't wise to say everything we think or feel. The most important question always is, what is it I wish to accomplish? If it is to preserve both the "I" and the "We," then we need to ask ourselves, "What is it I need to say or not to say?" Restraint is something we must be intentional about learning if we want to be at our best. When we talk about what is truly important to us, we must speak from a place of calm and conviction.

It is crucially important that we acknowledge the counterfeit to "speaking the truth" What is it not?

Speaking my truth is not:

- Exaggerating—"You always … You never … "
- Interrupting
- Blaming—"You make me feel stupid."
- Judgment—"You're overreacting."
- Name calling—"You're a jerk."
- Mind reading—"You meant to hurt me."
- Complaining endlessly as we continue to tolerate unsolicited advice
- Giving insults
- Being rude

Speaking the Truth is:

- Owning who we are
- What we need
- What we believe
- What we feel
- What our values are
- What our expectations are

What our limits are
What our goals are
Where we stand on certain issues
Asking questions so that we can better understand another's perspective.

Our safety and survival must not depend on our significant other, but be solidly established in Jesus Christ's love. Then we can think, speak, and act with clarity in our relationships. We can be intimate—we can allow ourselves to be known and we can deepen the experience of knowing another person. We can nurture our relationship and we can move towards our significant other in an honest, loving and generous way even in the face of disagreement. We can speak our truth, and we can welcome the other's expression of truth even if our perspectives are different.

Speaking our truth is a spiritual journey towards maturity.

ACTION STEP

Journal the answers to these questions:

Is my behavior in the midst of conflict or attack consistent with my stated values and beliefs? Give a recent example.

Who am I? (Describe yourself as a loving friend would describe you).

What are my needs?

What do I believe?

What are my values?

What are my expectations?

What are my goals?

What are my limits?

What do I think about?

When was the last time I moved towards someone when he or she disagreed with me?

"When one is out of touch with oneself, one cannot touch others."

ANNE MORROW LINDBERGH[37]

"Speaking the truth in love, we will in all things grow up into him who is the Head, that is, Christ"

(EPHESIANS 4:15).

"He who answers before listening—that is his folly and his shame"

(PROVERBS 18:13).

STEP #16

Know How to Say "No"

How many times have you felt cornered by a friend's request? "Can you come over?" "Will you help in the nursery on Sunday?" "Can I borrow that antique vase of your grandma's?"

Do you find it easy to say "No" to a friend, or do you struggle and eventually find yourself saying "Yes" when everything in you is screaming "No"?

Unless you are willing to say "No," your "Yes" is meaningless. It is compliance, not a statement of choice and willing agreement. When going along becomes the only way to get along, the approval we seek can be addictive.

Jesus Christ has this to say: "Simply let your 'Yes' be 'Yes,' and your 'No', 'No;' anything beyond this comes from the evil one" (Matthew 5:37).

Most of us fight our people-pleasing, dependent tendencies on an ongoing basis. The good news is, if we learn a few new skills, we will not say "Yes" when we really want to say "No."

SKILL # 1: LEARN TO DELAY YOUR ANSWER IN ORDER TO THINK THROUGH ALL YOUR OPTIONS.

"Everyone should be quick to listen, slow to speak" (James 1:19).

It's amazing how you will heighten your sense of personal control if you afford yourself the luxury of delay.

If someone makes a request by phone, say you will call the person back by such and such time—then do it. Let the person know that you need to check your schedule, or that you need time to carefully consider the request.

Ideally if the request happens in a face-to-face setting, excuse yourself to use the bathroom, make a telephone call, or get something from your car. Remove yourself physically so that you override your automatic impulse to please. We all need time to think before we commit ourselves to doing anything.

ACTION STEP

In your journal write down at least three statements that could buy time such as, "I need time to carefully consider your request." Memorize your statements and practice using them with someone who is on your inner strength team.

SKILL # 2: THE BROKEN RECORD TECHNIQUE. USE THIS SKILL WHEN YOU FACE RESISTANCE TO YOUR REQUEST FOR TIME.

Let your friend know that you have heard and understood both the request and your friend's emotional reaction to your need for time. Then repeat the same phrase you used in Skill # 1 to buy time. Be a broken record. Don't get caught giving excuses.

Friend: "I need you to do me a favor. You know I'm in charge of the graduation party at the high school. Will you give me half a day on Saturday to sell raffle tickets at the grocery store?"

You: "I need you to hold the line for a moment."

Friend: "Sure."

You: (Read the phrases you've written to buy time. Keep them by your phone. Select one.) "I might have a conflict on Saturday morning. I won't know for sure until tomorrow. I'll phone you back then."

Friend: "Can't you tell me now? It's a terrible pressure having to come up with volunteers."

You: "I hear your anxiety. I might have a conflict on Saturday morning. I won't know for sure until tomorrow. I'll phone you tomorrow." (Broken Record.)

Friend: "If you'd just commit for an hour it would help me out."

You: "Thank you for asking me. I might have a conflict on Saturday morning. I will call you tomorrow."

ACTION STEP

Identify one or two people who regularly ask you to do things. In fact, think back to a burdensome request made of you recently. Write out the script of what happened, but this time use the Broken Record Technique to buy yourself time.

SKILL # 3: USE THE SANDWICH TECHNIQUE WHEN YOUR ANSWER IS "NO."

Top slice:	A positive statement.
Filling:	Saying "No" to their request.
Bottom Slice:	A positive statement.

For example: "Thank you for the opportunity to help with raising money for grad night. It turns out I will not be able to help you this time, but I want to thank you for thinking I was capable of doing that."

Mean every word that you say. Don't lie, whine, apologize, or turn into a drama queen. Expect your friend to accept your "No." The sandwich technique is best delivered with a smile. Practice doing it.

Warning: If your friend attempts to change your mind, revert back to the Broken Record Technique with a statement like this: "I understand your disappointment. I have a conflict on Saturday morning. I will not be able to help you."

Avoid any further discussion or argument. Your "No" must be final.

ACTION STEP

In your journal write out a script using the Sandwich Technique for a request you were given in the past or one facing you today. Practice this technique with your inner strength group.

SKILL #4: THE COUNTEROFFER SANDWICH TECHNIQUE.

Top Slice: A negative statement saying "No" to the request.
Filling: A positive statement that provides an alternative suggestion.
Bottom Slice: A negative statement restating you cannot comply with the request.
For example: "I'm calling you back about Saturday morning. Unfortunately, I won't be able to be there all morning, but I could come for one hour. If that isn't helpful, I can't be there at all."

ACTION STEP

In your journal, prepare a counteroffer to a request someone has made of you recently. Practice giving this proposal.

Now is the time to put all of your new skills together. Create a script that can become your own.

1. Someone makes a request of you.
2. Excuse yourself or put her on hold.
3. Review your "Buying Time" statements.
4. Return to the conversation and buy time.
5. The person tries to pressure you into making an immediate decision.
6. Use the Broken Record Technique. Be firm and positive. Repeat it two or three times if necessary.
7. Call back and use the Sandwich Technique to say "No" or the Counteroffer Sandwich to present a counterproposal.
8. The person tries to pressure you again.
9. Respond with the Broken Record Technique.
10. Celebrate! You have learned the skills that enable you to say "No" in a firm, caring and positive manner.

"None of us will ever accomplish anything excellent or commanding, except when he listens to this whisper which is heard by him alone."

RALPH WALDO EMERSON[38]

"If the people you deal with know that you can say 'No', they will trust your 'Yes'!"

JANET CONGO

STEP #17

Study My Reactions

When Susan was a young girl she learned that her anger was not a welcomed part of who she was. On that fateful day she screamed at her brother. She had spent hours carefully constructing a block house for her stuffed animals when big brother, followed by the family dog, came racing full speed through the family room. Blocks went flying in every direction and Susan yelled.

Both of her parents came running into the room and both of them got in her face. She was given a litany of guilt messages. Scripture was quoted, she was banned from their presence to her room and forced to apologize to her brother. He was not even reprimanded.

She learned a strong message that day. Christians don't express anger, and if I want to be loved and accepted I won't either. After years of repressing this God-given emotion, of disowning the physical tension she seemed to experience continually, she stopped feeling any anger. In fact she prided herself on her restraint. That is, until she got married. How was it possible that she had married such an angry man? Their conflicts were getting uglier. She was saying things that she never dreamed would come out of her mouth. She knew that it was paramount that he get to a therapist. He needed to be fixed and she knew what he needed.

What happened in your home? What emotions were welcomed and what ones weren't? Who could be emotional and who couldn't? What emotions are you comfortable being in the presence of and which ones aren't you comfortable with?

What we don't know can hurt us. It can also hurt our loved ones.

A strong emotion doesn't disappear when we deny or disown it. It is still stuck under the surface; we just become disconnected from it. It's as if we've been given an emotional anesthetic. We feel very little. We are numb. As long as we stay isolated we can continue our charade of self-control; but when we are in an intimate relationship we often find that repressed emotion in our significant other. We also become aware of our own irritability, depression, anxiety, sickness, or erratic behavior.

Each of us has parts of ourselves that we are ashamed of and want to ignore. One of the reasons we need to study our reactions is that our reaction may be justified or it may be a projection. Just as a movie projects an image on a screen, I can project the feelings that I am fearful of or ashamed of onto the people I am closest to.

If we haven't owned our own anger, we will be critical of the anger of someone we love. Perhaps we haven't acknowledged our dependent and needy parts, so we pull away when our husband shows his needy side. How can we know that we are projecting? Our reaction is excessive given the circumstances. We overreact. Our rage and condemnation far exceeds the other's failings or mistake.

If we are willing to face reality, conflict can teach us so much. Take a Time Out the next time you find yourself furious at your significant other. Tell him that you want to discuss this issue, but first you need to understand your intense reaction. Commit to return to the conversation when you have calmed yourself down.

Open up your journal. Perhaps you are reacting because you don't feel heard or taken seriously. Rather than condemning yourself because you're an angry person, a lousy Christian, or a marital failure, listen non-judgmentally to your anger. When we feel an emotion that scares or disturbs us, we must learn to go with the emotion, to observe it, feel it, and let it teach us. Usually when we are angry, breathing is restricted and muscles are tense. Breathe deeply and relax your muscles, then write these two sentence completion exercises at the top of two journal pages, one on each page.

What is it I am upset at? (e.g., My husband isn't taking me seriously.)

If I <u>(do what he isn't doing, e.g., take him seriously)</u>, I would________.

If I (do what he isn't doing, e.g., take myself seriously),
I would ________________.

Keep adding additional endings as quickly as possible. Speed is essential. Don't think or censor what you are writing, just complete the sentences. If you go blank, invent possible endings. You might be surprised at what you learn.

Don't worry if your sentence completions are true, reasonable or profound. Study your answers. Did you learn anything?

Susan learned a lot when she did this exercise. She was upset that her husband wasn't taking her words seriously. At the top of her journal she wrote: If I took my husband seriously, I would:

Be a more active listener.
Let him know I heard him.
Let him know I sought out his perspective.
Look in his eyes when he was talking.
Be less preoccupied.
Affirm him more often.
Be less defensive.

At the top of the other page she wrote: If I took myself seriously, I would:

Listen to my gut.
Stop apologizing when I express an opinion or feeling or thought.
Speak up.
Stop apologizing for my mistakes.
Be open to a broader perspective than just mine.
Think before I speak.
Stop saying what I don't mean.
Be more aware.

You can only imagine how different the conversation with Susan's husband was after her Time Out for reflection than it would have been when all she was aware of was his inability to take her seriously.

When we study our reactions and non-judgmentally own our feelings, the exact opposite of what we most fear happens. Rather than being out of control emotionally, we discover a disowned or denied part of ourselves. The result is a new integrity and a wholeness that is the result of seeking the truth. We become more comfortable in our own skin with the knowledge that even our reactions have much to teach us about ourselves. Our self-esteem is strengthened.

Jesus asks each of us a profound question, "Why do you look at the speck of sawdust in your [significant other's] eye and pay no attention to the plank in your own eye?" (Matthew 7:3). If we are strangers to ourselves, others will be strangers to us.

ACTION STEP

1. Make a list of the qualities you do not like in other people. What gets under your skin?
2. Read your list and then underline the qualities that you not only dislike, but hate or despise.
3. Now do the sentence completion exercise in your journal.
   If I ________________ to my significant other,
   I would ______________.
   If I ______________ to myself, I would ___________.

What did you learn about yourself? Summarize your discoveries.

"Everything that irritates us about others can lead us to an understanding of ourselves."

CARL JUNG[39]

STEP #18

Master My Anger!

The most popular and roughest contact sport in the country is not football—it is marriage. Behind the closed doors of our homes, precious children of God who give free reign to their anger cause incredible damage. They corrode self-esteem, undermine trust, breed resentment, anxiety, sleep difficulties, and depression. Anger blocks insight because for a temporary time we lose our ability to see the good in the other person. Often we negatively label another's motivations and actions, resulting in inaccurate interpretations of actual events. Sometimes the more we blame and criticize, the more justified we feel. Anger begets more anger and the end result is that love is damaged and we end up feeling either self-righteous and superior, or guilty and shamed. What an incredible waste of time for precious children of God, created in His image who have been put on earth to love and encourage each other.

According to the Scripture, anger is a normal, God-given emotion to protect love. Ephesians 4:26 challenges us, "In your anger, do not sin." If our anger destroys love, then is it sin.

It is inevitable that in intimate relationships and close friendships we will feel angry. The truth is we are never persuasive when we are abrasive. When we hurt the other person, we lose sight of their value, of our value and we attempt to create distance. Paradoxically people who attempt to over control their anger produce out-of-control eruptions. None of us builds our self-esteem by losing control of our tongue and by annihilating someone else. Solomon writes, "A fool gives full vent to his anger, but a wise [woman] keeps [herself] under control" (Proverbs

29:11). We all must set an anger ceiling on ourselves.

Is it possible to master our anger? Yes, it is. We must learn to use the Time Out tool effectively in order to master anger. Perhaps at one point in your history, you played a team sport like volleyball, soccer, softball, or basketball. If so, you are familiar with the concept. Coaches use Time Outs to accomplish specific purposes: to educate the team, give the team members an attitude adjustment, help them refocus, help them settle down, break the offensive rhythm of the other team, and to help the players pace themselves. We need Time Outs for exactly the same reasons.

In order to be effective in potential conflict situations, we need to become extremely adept at using the strategy of Time Out. After all, none of us benefit when our tongue licks us. Here are six steps to an effective Time Out.

1. Call a time out as soon as you are aware that you or the other person is beginning to lose control. Feelings are beginning to escalate. Increased voice volume, hostile language, aggressive, animated and accusatory gestures are all signs of escalation. If you are aware of your heart racing, or are feeling frightened or overwhelmed or on the defensive, do not attempt to talk. Instead ask for a Time Out. The purpose of a Time Out is to detach temporarily so that you can attach lovingly at a later time.

2. Own the truth that you need to calm down to better be able to stay on task and to deal with the real issue at hand. A Time Out is about you and what you need. It is not about telling the other person that he or she is out of control.

ACTION STEP

How Do I Ask for a Time Out?

Create an exit line that tells the other person you will be leaving for a specific amount of time to calm down and think. Commit to return at an agreed upon time to resume the discussion (e.g. In an hour, or after dinner). Here are three examples of exit techniques:

"I need to leave to control the only thing I can control, which is myself and my anger."

"I am leaving because I don't want to regret the words I might say in anger."

"I am leaving because I need an attitude adjustment and some time to think."

---

3. Use the Broken Record Technique with no apologies. If the other person resists your attempts to leave and tries to provoke you further, what do you do?

A. Leave physically, or if that is impossible, leave by refusing to engage in conversation.
B. What do I do when I leave? Cool down, gain personal control and analyze. We want to disconnect our automatic search and destroy radar. We want our perspective to broaden so that we aren't succumbing to tunnel vision. We want to counteract our very natural tendency to detach and to withdraw love when someone displeases us. We want to understand our reaction to this issue. We need to ask ourselves, "What is it we really want or need? Is there any way that our choices are creating problems for the other person?" This is the time for journaling. Be certain that you can verbalize your position on paper prior to attempting to verbalize it in person.

Not only is it necessary to ask these questions, it is also important as Christ's followers to stop and analyze our reaction. Healthy anger, an anger motivated by powerful love, gets angry at certain things while unhealthy anger gets angry at other things and is deceived.

Healthy Anger (Powerful Love) Gets angry at:	Unhealthy Anger Gets angry at:
Withdrawal of Love	Being held accountable
Irresponsibility	Independent Choices

Restriction of Freedom
Condemnation
Control
Disagreement
Attempts to Influence

4. What happens when I return to the relationship? The bottom line intention with a Time Out is to resolve the issue. It is effective to ask the other person if he or she is ready to discuss the issue when you return. If it is not a good time for the other person, honor that and ask him or her to verbalize when a good time would be. Make an appointment to discuss the issue.

If in the process of talking about this topic, your anger starts to bubble again you may need to call another Time Out in order to get yourself in a better place. It may help to implement a 24-hour rule. Any topic that causes extreme irritation in either of you gets a 24-hour cooling off period before you discuss it again. Set another appointment time. It may be helpful to discuss it in a public place, because then you will both work harder at not raising your voices.

The verse, "Do not let the sun go down while you are still angry" (Ephesians 4:26) doesn't mean that all issues need to be resolved by sunset. It means diffuse your anger, don't let it drag into the next day and the next unresolved. Don't withdraw from each other for days or weeks at a time. Jesus never withdraws His love or presence when we displease Him.

The tool of Time Out helps us to own our own anger and to effectively communicate our truth. Our intention must be to address what we would like to see changed in our relationship while staying attached to the person with whom we are upset.

When we are angry, we face so many choices. We can attack, antagonize, avoid, or attach. If we master our anger with the help of Time Outs, anger will help us reach goals, solve problems, and protest anything that is destructive to love. It will protect freedom, love, and attachment. It will raise and solidify our self-esteem and the esteem of the one with whom we are upset. It opens the door so we can honestly share our truth with them.

"Speak when you are angry and you will make
the best speech you will ever regret."
AMBROSE BIERCE[40]

"Anyone can become angry. That is easy.
But to be angry with the right person, to the right degree,
at the right time for the right purpose and in the right way,
That is not easy."
ARISTOTLE[41]

STEP #19

Embrace Reality

How many people do you know who imagine that they are in love with someone and yet ignore that person or are repeatedly unkind? It is too easy to comfort ourselves with a fantasy rather than owning up to reality. Where there is no self-awareness or self-examination we end up living a contradiction. We must begin with what is, not what we wish could be or what we think should be.

If we don't begin with reality, self-esteem is undermined and anxiety increased. Yet it is far easier at times to avoid reality than to embrace a conscious reality. Sometimes we avoid conscious awareness by telling ourselves that we are too tired or too busy to act or think, or by choosing to be passive or lazy. This choice leaves us feeling inadequate and incompetent. Other times we surrender to the emotion of the moment rather than observing our feelings, experiencing them, studying them, and choosing whether we act on those emotions. We avoid reality when we lose awareness of how this moment is important to the big picture. We must be in the moment, but not trapped by the moment.[42]

Teeth marks on our tongue may be a sign of both maturity and a reality-based awareness. It's all too easy for us to choose to be diverted from the reality of the moment by an irrelevant issue. Even a humorous comment can help us escape the reality we need to confront. Cleaning and organizing cupboards can seem so important when there is a manuscript to be completed.

We commit ourselves to blindness rather than awareness if we believe that we must never make a mistake or that our worth is somehow diminished if we make an error. Reality-based self-esteem requires an eagerness to discover, face, and admit our mistakes. Correcting mistakes is far more satisfying than pretending they didn't happen or covering up the fact that they did.

Reality is not the enemy. Choosing to live blindly—that is the enemy. When we choose to sleep walk through life we have good reason to be afraid. Nathaniel Branden puts it this way: "The tragedy of many lives is that we make the most fateful decisions with little or no awareness that our choices will change the shape and direction of our existence . . . . We are ruled more by impulse or routine or conformity to convention than by rational reflection."[43]

The question we need to ask ourselves on a daily basis is, "Today did I show up? Did I bring a focused, disciplined, intentional consciousness to my life and the people and experiences in it? Or did I live mechanically, in a trancelike state that was neither aware or mindful?"

In order to have a reality-based, healthy sense of self, our values, goals, and actions must be aligned. The choice to live consciously, responsibly, and with integrity must be practiced intentionally and regularly. We are each responsible for living so that our thinking, values, and reality are not in contradiction.

It is too easy to give away pieces of our soul every day in order to "belong" or to "fit in." Doing that diminishes self-esteem. It is too easy to get complacent and reject any new information that might result in having to modify our course or correct our assumptions. When we settle for such a non-thinking approach to life, self-esteem shrivels.

Self-esteem does not grow as a result of looking in a mirror and telling ourselves that we are "good enough, smart enough, and doggone-it, people like us" as the Stuart Smalley character used to do on "Saturday Night Live." We can't attain self-esteem by working harder, acquiring more possessions, seeking after praise, boasting, arrogance, sexual conquests or eating, drinking or drugging ourselves into a non-thinking state. Faking reality is not the recipe for increased self-assurance.

Self-esteem is enhanced when we choose to live in accordance with reality; when we take responsibility for what is ours; when we believe that with God's help and the support of our inner strength team, we are capable of learning what we need in order to face whatever life brings us;

when we are intentional about matching our value system and our goals and behavior. These choices take both awareness and perseverance.

ACTION STEP

Answer these questions in your journal.

If one of my goals is to have satisfying relationships, what shape are my significant relationships in now? How would those closest to me rate me as a friend or a mate? Are there frustrations and unresolved issues in my intimate relationships that I have been avoiding? If so, what intentional steps do I need to take toward resolution? How far am I from my aspirations? What intentional steps do I need to take to move closer to my dreams?

Who am I? What do I want? Where am I going? What are my values? What are my goals? How are my actions in alignment with my values and goals? If they aren't, what can I do to correct that?

When I embrace consciously whatever reality gives me, when I live by my convictions, when I speak up when it is warranted, and remain silent when my comment will serve no higher purpose, when I do my best, take responsibility for my actions and my mistakes, when I persevere when persevering is difficult, I will have consciously embraced reality. As a result, my self-esteem will be strengthened. I will be authentic.

"We must be willing to get rid of the life we've planned, so as to have the life that is waiting for us."

JOSEPH CAMPBELL[44]

STEP #20

Promote Change Positively

We are each capable of destroying trust and love in our relationships when we got into a control mode. Our significant other may comply but we will lose his heart. Guilt messages such as "if you really loved me, you'd … " are meant to make our friend bad for making a separate choice. Anger isn't far behind guilt. Again we are furious that this person's separateness is a threat to our comfort. Some of us don't yell, we just nag. The dictionary defines "nagging" as, "persistent petty faultfinding, scolding, or urging." Others of us argue, plead, and push until our mate retreats in a state of exhaustion and frustration. The most powerful attempt to control happens when we disconnect emotionally from our mate in order to give a strong punishing message. *How dare you be separate?* we scream internally. We withhold love or sex until the other person sees things from our perspective. Outright judgment and condemnation ooze from our pores.

If we are going to promote change positively, we must learn to value the other person's freedom. Allow him time and room to grow. Allow for thoughts, feelings, questions, and opinions. At times we just have to grieve that we are not going to get it our way. Grieving is sad; it has no anger or control in it.

We must take the time to rid ourselves of any judgmentalism, condemnation, or pride. Replace these things with mercy. Remember, we all fall short of God's ideal. As Paul writes, "If someone is caught in a sin, you who are spiritual should restore him gently. But watch yourself, or you also may be tempted. Carry each other's burdens and in this way you will fulfill the law of Christ" (Galatians 6:1–2).

Love the person, but be honest about how the other's choices affect you. Use "I" statements. Continue to communicate your support and your encouragement. Guard against any spirit of one-upmanship. Connect with empathy if anyone is hurting. If necessary, set boundaries. "I want to discuss this with you. I need to take a Time Out for 30 minutes because I'm so upset. I will try again at that time."

Use this time to get in touch with yourself. Own your own feelings, wishes, thoughts, and beliefs. If your mate has pointed out something that he would like you to work on, don't get defensive. Value the other's input enough to think about it, pray about it, and examine it. If you aren't sure about the validity of the issue get feedback from honest, loving, supportive people. If after doing that you still can't own it, let it go.

Growth rarely is easy. Change is not comfortable. The familiar pattern, even if totally destructive, always feels more familiar. It can feel right even if it is wrong. Others are only free to change when we stop trying to force it. If we promote change positively, we will discover that we have experienced growth too. We will be boundary lovers. We will respect the person we are becoming.

ACTION STEP

Journal about a recent time when someone, in separateness, did something that hurt you. What was your first response? If you are like me, your initial response is not to grieve, but to be angry. Write a few sentences about the grief you experienced. Then write a positive request. ("It would mean a lot to me if you would attend my daughter's wedding.") We can't say that we value people and their freedom if we don't value their decisions.

"When you're through changing, you're through!"

BRUCE BARTON[45]

STEP #21

Accept Responsibility for My Own Happiness

Have you noticed how many women seem dissatisfied? When we were little girls, our mother was the secret to our happiness. If she provided what we wanted, we were happy. If not, we'd let her know about our displeasure. Very few mothers told us that they weren't responsible for our state of mind. That was an inside job—our job.

Many of us have gotten in the habit of waiting. "Someday my prince will come." "Someday my breasts will come." We see ourselves as the victim of circumstances. We blame others for our current state of affairs. Marriage certainly isn't the utopia many of us envisioned, so we have a baby and then another, always waiting for happiness and fulfillment.

After years of delayed fulfillment, " I will be happy when ..." becomes a nostalgic, "I was happy when ... Those truly were the best years of my life." Many women live the first half of their adult lives postponing satisfaction and the last half with regrets. It's as if we're secretly waiting for someone to come to our rescue. That fantasy is dangerous because as a result of it, we stay passively resentful rather than actively choosing happiness.

ACTION STEP

In your journal complete these sentences:
I'd be a much happier person if ...
I contribute to my own lack of happiness by ...

Many of us have discovered that when we get our glass slipper, it doesn't fit. Happiness is a choice. It is not a destination, it is a journey. "This is the day the LORD has made; let us rejoice and be glad in it" (Psalm 118:24). Happiness takes an act of the will. (If you can't choose happiness, you may be suffering from a biochemical disorder. Please go and see both your medical doctor and a therapist.)

God is at work in our lives, but God will not do what we must do. We must choose contentment. When life presents us with lemons, we must learn to make lemonade. Each of us must let go of the fantasy that others are responsible for our happiness. We must choose satisfaction now over the philosophy of "I'll be happy when ..." Don't let your tombstone read, "Lived 90 years. Died at 32 years of age." How would your life be different if you chose happiness now?

ACTION STEP

Review these quotes on happiness made by others.

> "You're happiest while you're making the greatest contribution."
> ROBERT KENNEDY[46]

> "One thing I know;
> the only ones among you who will be really happy
> are those who will have sought and found how to serve."
> ALBERT SCHWEITZER[47]

> "If you want to be happy, set yourself a goal that commands your thoughts, liberates your energy, and inspires your hopes. Happiness is within you. It comes from doing some certain thing into which you can put all your thought and energy. If you want to be happy, get enthusiastic about something."
> DALE CARNEGIE[48]

> "Happiness lies in the joy of achievement and the thrill of creative effort."
> FRANKLIN D. ROOSEVELT[49]

"The secret of happiness is not in doing what one likes, but in liking what one does."

J.M. BARRIE[50]

"The secret of happiness is to count your blessings, not your birthdays."

SHANNON ROSE[51]

"Our happiness depends on the habit of mind we cultivate. So practice happy thinking everyday. Cultivate the merry heart, develop the happiness habit, and life will be a continual feast."

NORMAN VINCENT PEALE[52]

"It is not how much we have, but how much we enjoy, that makes happiness."

CHARLES SPURGEON[53]

"We have all been placed on this earth to discover our own path, and we will never be happy if we live someone else's idea of life."

JAMES VAN PRAAGH[54]

"The grand essentials to happiness in this life are something to do, someone to love and something to hope for."

JOSEPH ADDISON[55]

"I have found that most people are about as happy as they make up their minds to be."

ABRAHAM LINCOLN[56]

Has your perspective on happiness changed as a result of reading these quotes? Explain.

Happiness is a Choice!

STEP #22

Find My Inner Playmate!

"God is a comedian whose audience is afraid to laugh."

H.L. MENCKEN[57]

When was the last time you laughed so hard that you could barely catch your breath? When did you kick off those sensible loafers, dance up a storm, jump on a trampoline, or have a late night on the town with three of your closest friends? If you can't remember, you may be fun-impaired! Fun begins with our willingness to seek it and seize it. We have to take time off from worrying, soul-searching, and trying so hard. We must stop taking ourselves so seriously. We must coax out that long-ignored inner playmate so that even the most mundane moments can be transformed into treasures. It's a wasted day if laughter has been absent from it.

Two years ago my husband and I took out my 85-year-old mentor for dinner and a movie. Concerned about her stamina, we asked her to choose the time for the movie. With sparkling eyes she said, "Let's go to the late movie. It's been years since I've been out past midnight."

Are you fun to be around? Do you approach life with a sense of humor? Do you see the bright side of things even in the midst of difficulties? Or are you one of those people who live sensibly hour by hour, day after day?

Many of us have to be intentional about welcoming our inner playmate. While we're intent on proving our value to the world, we rarely give ourselves permission to have fun. After all, that is wasting time; we should be accomplishing something worthwhile.

A friend who had to give herself permission to have fun found it helpful to put the vacuum cleaner in the middle of the floor before escaping to go for a bike ride with her two children. That way if someone dropped by it would appear as if she was in the middle of an "important" task. Do whatever it takes to cure yourself of the compulsion to prove your value every second. Jesus Christ has affirmed your value separate from your accomplishments.

When girls are about 10 or 11 years of age, they begin to retreat inside themselves. They begin to lose their audacity, their boisterousness, and their independence. They try not to stand out in the crowd—to be too much! With that decision, they severely limit their ability to enjoy life. With that choice, they invite depression into their life. It is just a matter of time until they start to substitute counterfeit fun for healthy pleasures. Counterfeit pleasures help them avoid the tough realities of life. Healthy fun renews them and helps them face those realities. It brings balance to their emotional lives. A physician, Mark Epstein put it this way: "Like breathing and dreaming, play serves a homeostatic function. Like a thermostat, it kicks in when the internal environment is too hot or too cold and brings things into a more tolerable balance."[58]

Counterfeit pleasures leave us dissatisfied. We must increase our consumption of the counterfeit in order to achieve the same level of pleasure. Healthy fun isn't boring. In fact healthy fun leaves us invigorated and refreshed, rather than full of regrets, shame, and emptiness.

Life is far more sacred and miraculous than any of us can ever imagine. We don't get any instant replays. Our task and privilege is to live consciously, to participate as deeply and fully as we are capable of and to enjoy life's wonders.

Helen Keller, who was struck deaf and blind at the age of two, wrote these words:

> Life is either a daring adventure … or nothing at all! I, who cannot see, find hundreds of things to interest mere touch. I feel the delicate symmetry of a leaf. I pass my hands lovingly about the smooth skin of a silver birch or the rough shaggy bark of a pine. I feel the delightful, velvety texture of a flower and discover

> its remarkable convolutions and something of the miracle of nature is revealed to me. Occasionally, if I'm fortunate, I can place my hand gently on a small tree and feel the happy quiver of a bird in full song. At times, my heart cries out, longing to see these things. But if I can get so much pleasure in mere touch, how much more beauty must be revealed by sight. Yet, those who have eyes apparently see little. The panorama of color and action which fill the world are taken for granted. It is a great pity that in the world of light the gift of sight is used only as a mere convenience, rather than as a means of adding fullness.[59]

How much joy and laughter can you stand? Lee Ann Womack has an amazing song out on the country-western charts, a song that she wrote for her young daughter. One of the lines in it challenges her daughter to choose to dance rather than choosing to sit out the dance. Have you settled for being a wallflower, sleep-walking through life or are you a mentally, physically, emotionally, and spiritually active participant in life?

ACTION STEP

In your journal answer these questions.

If your life were to come to an abrupt end tomorrow what would you regret not doing today? Why?

What did you love to do as a child to have fun? How could you make space in your life for some of those activities today?

Which of your friends really knows how to have fun? Is there anything you could learn from that person? Explain.

Which movies really make you laugh? Start a list. Ask others to add to your list. Watch some of them.

What are your favorite active things that you do to have fun or that you would like to do?

"Blessed is she who has learned to laugh at herself, for she will never cease to be entertained."

JOHN POWELL[60]

STEP #23

Choose to See Possibilities

If you always think the way you always thought, you will always get what you always got. If you always do what you always did, you will always get what you always got. The road to despair is paved with cynicism, sarcasm, pessimism, passivity, despair, and jealousy.

People who see a glass as half-empty are talking fantasy. Half-full is a measure of physical reality. The optimist deals with reality, the pessimist doesn't.

Our God is a positive God. The Bible is Good News. The cross is the ultimate plus sign. What is your focus?

Religion or relationship?
Doubt or faith?
Fear or hope?
Sin or salvation?
Regret or discipline?
Yesterday or today?
Negative or positive?
Crisis or challenge?
Reacting or responding?
Taking chances or making choices?
Impossibilities or possibilities?
Failures or successes?
Blaming or blooming?
Criticizing or creating?

Nightmares or dreams?
Analyzing or affirmation?

When you look in the mirror do you focus on what is wrong or do you notice the things you like? Do you view yourself and others as people who are in the process of becoming? Choose to focus on what the Lord has done in your life rather than on the part not yet finished. Praise and thanksgiving will spring from your lips.

Jesus Christ opened up a world of possibility in which each person has intrinsic value and worth, where acceptance replaces condemnation, where we can do all things through Christ who strengthens us.

If we operate out of Christ's value system rather than our culture's, no one will be made wrong, no one will be stabbed in the back by careless words, and there will be no distinction between "us" and "them." In this environment transformation is possible.

OPERATING IN THE REALM OF POSSIBILITY

> A little girl in second grade underwent chemotherapy for leukemia. When she returned to school, she wore a scarf to hide the fact that she had lost all of her hair. But some of the children pulled it off, and in their nervousness laughed and made fun of her. The little girl was mortified at that. She begged her mother not to make her return to school. Her mother tried to encourage her, saying, "The other children will get used to it, and any way your hair will grow in again soon."
>
> The next morning, when their teacher walked into class, all the children were sitting in their seats, some still tittering about the girl who had no hair. "Good morning, children," the teacher said, smiling warmly in her familiar way. She took off her coat and scarf. Her head was completely shaved.
>
> After that, a rash of children begged their parents to let them shave their heads. And when a child came to class with short hair, newly bobbed, all the children laughed merrily—not out of fear—but out of the joy of the game. And everybody's hair grew back at the same time.[61]

Just like that teacher, Jesus has released each of us from our shame and embarrassment because of what has happened to us. Baldness becomes possibility—"a fashion statement, an act of choice, a game to play, and an opportunity for solidarity and connection. No one was made wrong. There was nothing to fix."[63] So everything in your life becomes possibility as a result of Christ's transforming power.

As Christian women we must hold out the truth of possibility. We must not lose hope. Why? Because where God is, there is always hope. Do you believe that "all things work together for good to those who love God?" If you do, the result will be a positive belief, affirming that good will be the result of everything happening in life. Learning to accept your realities and working with them is the outward sign of your inward hope. Do you demand that people or circumstances must change in order for you to be happy? There is a heavenly reason for everything in life: may we always learn and grow from our experiences.

This doesn't mean we should say we don't have any problems. Neither does it mean we should expect to be happy in the midst of difficult circumstances. It does mean we can positively affirm that there are no circumstances in our lives that we cannot use for growth. Purpose, commitment, and vision—the very essence of possibility can come out of any circumstance if we choose to embrace rather than resist it, if we choose creativity instead of reactivity.

ACTION STEP

Answer this question in your journal:

Is there a situation in my life right now that I need to bring the mindset of possibility to? Write about it.

"A life isn't significant except for its impact on other lives."

JACKIE ROBINSON[63]

STEP #24

Serve Out of Love, Not Duty

The interdependent woman finds her identify first as a result of Jesus Christ's loving sacrifice for her and next through loving God and others. Her self-fulfillment comes as a by-product of loving service. The woman who accepts this as her life's direction will find she is walking a holy walk, not always easy or popular, but always growth-producing. She will discover she is walking in her Savior's footsteps. In Philippians 2:5–8, Paul exhorts us: "Your attitude should be the same as that of Christ Jesus: Who, being in very nature God, did not consider equality with God something to be grasped, but made himself nothing, taking the very nature of a servant, being made in human likeness. And being found in appearance as a man, he humbled himself and became obedient to death—even death on a cross!"

SERVE AS CHRIST SERVED

Our minds, so often self-centered, can hardly comprehend the fact that the Creator God of the universe would be willing to take on the form of a servant. But that is exactly what He did. He was willing to leave the comfort and honor of heaven to walk through the dust of this earth, to serve the disciples by washing their feet, and to rub shoulders with religious and irreligious humanity—who not only didn't believe He was God, but who contemptuously ridiculed Him. He, our God, chose to walk straight to His death on a tree that He had created at the hands of people He had created.

Our Lord was also a serving Lord after His resurrection. Christ was on the shore of Lake Galilee, cooking breakfast for seven exhausted disciples who had toiled all night trying to catch fish. A change in His status did not mean a change in His service. Truly Jesus Christ was among us as one who serves (see Luke 22:27). In the first three chapters of the Book of Revelation we discover that the risen Lord is the sovereign servant of the Church even today.

SERVE WITH A SECURE IDENTITY

As we begin to follow in our Master's footsteps, we learn that a commitment to servanthood is preceded by a strong sense of identity. Jesus was sure of His identity. He was God! John 10:30 records Christ's words, "I and the Father are one." He didn't have to grasp for deity, He was God. Because He was sure of His identity, He laid aside His position and willingly became human.

We, as interdependent Christian women, also have a strong sense of identity. We know we are highly significant to God and deeply loved by God. We know we are forgiven and accepted by God because of Jesus Christ's sacrifice and the Holy Spirit's power in us. We don't have to grasp for deity as Satan and Adam and Eve did. We face that tendency in ourselves. We never lose sight of knowing we are God's children. Because we are sure of this identity, we can choose to lay aside our rights and willingly become a servant of God and of others.

SERVE WITH A FULL HEART

Apart from the Holy Spirit within us, we give in order to receive, we love in order to be loved, and we forgive in order to be forgiven. Servanthood must be the result of the fullness of Christ within us. The story of Mary and Martha (Luke 10:38–42) serves as a reminder that our service exists as a result of the fullness of God within us. Otherwise it will be nothing but a duty, an obligation—and a real pain.

We've all been there, haven't we? We've served because we felt it was expected of us, because we wanted to be loved and appreciated, because we wanted to be served in return. It wasn't exactly a joy, was it? We didn't find any fulfillment in it, did we? Fulfillment never results when our loving and serving is motivated by self. Rather, fulfillment is the result of worshiping our Lord through our service. Peter must have encountered this begrudging attitude because in 1 Peter 4:9 he admonishes the Christians to "offer hospitality to one another without grumbling."

If servanthood is indeed our calling, we need to be constantly asking God to fill all of us with all of Him. We need to be filling our minds and spirits with Scripture, with prayer and meditation. We also need times to focus on the wonder of who God is. Worship releases us from self-centeredness and shows us that freedom comes from dependence on Jesus Christ. Joy is found there. As we spend quality time worshiping the risen Christ and delving deeper into the truth of God's Word, we will adopt a servant lifestyle.

Servanthood is the way we identify with our Christ. In Ephesians 5:1–2 we read this command: "Be imitators of God, therefore, as dearly loved children and live a life of love, just as Christ loved us and gave himself up for us, a fragrant offering and sacrifice to God." In Christ's value system "the greatest among you will be your servant" (Matthew 23:11). We are called to be imitators of our servant Lord rather than status-seekers in the world's system. As we give precedence to God's plan and words in our lives we will discover the truth of finding ourselves through losing ourselves.

SERVICE'S ATTITUDE!

Even though we affirm, as interdependent women, that others are our equals as we are their equals, we acknowledge that as Christ's servants we set aside our equal rights. We willingly, voluntarily become servants to one another in the body of Christ because we are identifying with our Lord.

Jesus was equal with God, but He didn't cling to His rights. He was willing to risk servanthood so our needs would be met as a result of His sacrifice. He loved us enough to serve us. Can we truly comprehend that statement? Rather than pouting over what He was giving up, Christ chose to concentrate on the people to whom He was giving. Can we do less? He laid aside His rights and submitted to His Father's plan. The result came to life when Jesus, the Creator God, knelt in front of mere humans and washed their feet.

One time an admirer asked Leonard Bernstein which instrument was the most difficult to play. Bernstein's answer is classic. "Second fiddle. I can get plenty of first violinists but to find one who plays second violin with as much enthusiasm or second French horn or second flute, now that's a problem. And yet if no one plays second we have no harmony."[64] This illustration hits home because I know how often I find myself building the kingdom of Jan, how often I like the front-row seats, how often I enjoy being center stage and how often I am self-conscious as opposed to God-conscious. The Holy Spirit is actively teaching me lessons about enthusiastically playing second violin. How's the harmony in your home and office?

SERVE BY USING WORDS CAREFULLY

Christ demonstrated His availability through His use of words. Do we bring a consciousness to our relationships by using our words wisely? Our words can draw someone near or they can drive someone away. They can undergird or undercut, bolster or belittle, demonstrate respect or disrespect. Words indicate whether we are more concerned with kindness or with always being correct; whether we are more interested in a ministry of reconciliation or in keeping a record of wrongs; whether we are more interested in lecturing or listening; whether we consider it necessary to be responsible for another person's actions or responsible for loving another person; whether our children, husbands, or friends are our friends or our foes. Words can encourage or enrage, affirm or attack, betray excitement or exhaustion, demonstrate concern or criticism. They can welcome or wound.

When an acquaintance arrives unexpectedly, your husband arrives home, or your children come home from school, what attitudes do your words convey? When you are in the middle of an errand, what do your words and attitude indicate to other people about your availability? Our words betray, as little else does, the value we put on availability. Our attitudes are also highly contagious. Like the measles, they reproduce themselves a hundredfold in our lives and spread into the world around us. Before we speak, it would be wise for us to ask ourselves, "Am I willing to live with the reality that I will create if I use my words in this way?"

SERVE ACTIVELY!

You've heard the saying that the darker the night is, the brighter the stars shine. We are called to be the bright shining stars in our homes, communities, and churches. Love is the evidence that we are Christ's women, called to be in partnership with our Lord in reaching our world.

Even though Christ is the initiator of love while we are the responders, this does not give us license to be passive responders to life. Dependence on our Savior alone frees us to be the most courageous lovers and servants of our world. In Romans 12:10–13 we read these words: "Be devoted to one another in brotherly love. Honor one another above yourselves. Never be lacking in zeal, but keep your spiritual fervor, serving the Lord. Be joyful in hope, patient in affliction, faithful in prayer."

SERVE HOSPITABLY

Do you associate the word hospitality with a spectacular table set with fresh flowers, candles, matching china, crystal, and sterling silver? I enjoy the beauty of those things, but that is not what I am referring to when I use the word "hospitality." I am referring to an *attitude* of being receptive and open to people, including my family, friends, and even strangers. It involves a willingness to see others from God's point of view as highly significant, deeply loved and valuable in spite of what they do, how they act, or what they look like. It involves acknowledging that everything I have, own, and am comes from God's hands. It becomes a willingness to share God's blessings with others. Obedience is involved and Paul challenges us to "accept one another, then, just as Christ accepted you, in order to bring praise to God" (Romans 15:7).

A very wise person once pointed out that the world is full of either guests or hosts. It seems to me the difference between the two is our willingness to make the world a beautiful place, both physically and emotionally, for other people. Without the cross of Jesus Christ we would all be guests. Only that cross transforms us into hosts.

How gentle the Holy Spirit has been with this goal-oriented woman, in molding me into a hospitable woman. I certainly was not always willing to be part of the process. When I was a new bride I really wanted to spend all my time with this new husband of mine. He had come from a home that was constantly full of people. I, on the other hand, had come from a home that entertained only a few times a year because of my mother's career plus the responsibility of being a pastor's wife and mother. Since Dave was used to a house full of people, he thought it was a little quiet with just the two of us. So with my husband as a motivator I started to entertain. What a spread I put on! What a table I set! Trouble was, by the time our friends arrived I was not only exhausted but had usually experienced one or two blow-ups with my hubby. I was not very interested in my guests' emotional state when they arrived. But I certainly wanted their compliments.

Would you believe the next year the Lord placed us in a pastorate? There I was—a minister's wife who viewed people as interruptions. You see, I had a college teaching job for the first time and I wanted to excel at it. At the same time we entertained mostly young people and I found myself doing it a great deal. It couldn't be spectacular because we just couldn't afford to feed multitudes that way. I was miserable. I was lonely. I resented the time I didn't have with my husband because of all his church responsibilities. It got so bad I felt I was wasting my time if I spent time talking on the phone.

Eventually we moved on to another position and God in His goodness sent an angel. The woman's name was Irene, and she helped the selfish, angry child in me. Dear Irene, such a gift of hospitality you rarely see. Irene always had time. If you arrived at her home first thing in the morning or late at night she was genuinely glad to see you. If you surprised her, after an initial comment about the state of affairs in her home, she would focus on you as if you were the most important person in her world. She entertained creatively but simply and she wasn't afraid to let you help. People were her main focus.

I was mightily impressed by the fact that Irene was as hospitable to her own family as she was to others. This was not a lady who had nothing to do. In fact, what she accomplished often made my head spin. But people were her focus and she loved us with an accepting, affirming servant love. As you can guess, Christians and non-Christians alike flocked to her, and the Holy Spirit used her to begin a work in me.

Slowly I began to change one thing at a time. The first thing I did was change my menus. Every experience didn't have to be gourmet. Whatever I prepared I attempted to have it completed 20 minutes before our guests were to arrive so Dave and I could pray for our friends and the evening. The result of those two decisions was miraculous. If the food couldn't be ready early I learned how to ask for help. What a concept!

That was the turning point in my life. I now believe that relationships are the most important thing in my world. In fact, I've been told I have the gift of hospitality and I think I do. But I know it's a gift that's been created in me by a loving heavenly Father who cares desperately about His children's relationships.

Perhaps you are naturally a people person. What a wonderful characteristic to have! A people person likes to be around people much of the time and she chooses when she will be alone. An introvert likes to be alone and chooses when she will be with people. Regardless of our natural inclinations, we are all called to serve through the vehicle of hospitality.

One summer we worshiped with a precious group of Christians in Fort Collins, Colorado. On the wall of their multi-purpose auditorium hung a huge banner. The words caught my attention and pulled on my heartstrings: "This is a healing place where inspiration, rest, the love of Christ and the praise of God will lift men's hearts and save their souls."

Dear Lord Jesus, in my attitudes, in my home, through my words, make me a healing place to which people come. That is hospitality. That is servanthood.

For your Holy Spirit, God,
I'm thankful!
Without Him, I'm nervous, anxious, fearful—too often thinking
of me:

What will she think of me?
How will I impress him?
Will they think I'm weird?
What if they don't like my idea?

But oh, how happy I am with your Holy Spirit!
He focuses my thoughts on You:
How may I best represent Jesus?
Will I be careful of His reputation?
What will be their response to His love through me?

Release! Support! Affirmation!
And then comes His serendipity!
In each person He shares with me
He reveals His Son.
He enables me to enjoy their differences!
Because of what He paid for them;
Because of what He's doing within them;
Because He's promised to finish
What He's started in each who chooses Him,
I can love them—
Actually enjoy them—
Each unique, special creation.

Thanks much, Lord,
For replacing my fear
With your love,
My anxiety with enjoyment,
My doubt with hope.

Your Spirit is my stronghold!
He is my treasure, my precious friend.[65]

ACTION STEP

In your journal, record your answers to these questions.

When I look at my attitude, would I call myself a guest or host? Give concrete examples.

When is hospitality a joy and when is it a drudgery? What makes the difference?

What is one step I could take that would move me in the direction of being a host?

"When people are serving, life is no longer meaningless."

JOHN GARDNER[66]

STEP #25

Stimulate My Dreams

"If I were to wish for anything I should not wish for wealth and power, but for the passionate sense of what can be, for the eye, which, ever young and ardent, sees the possible. Pleasure disappoints, possibility never. … "

SØREN KIERKEGAARD[67]

When you wake up in the middle of the night, what kind of dreaming or creative imagining do you do? Who is it that you want to become? What kind of a contribution do you want to make? Dreams happen in the space between what's here and what might be.

What are your hopes for the future? Define them. Have you wanted to go back to school but just not had the courage? What about the dream of going into business for yourself? Have you wanted to learn a new language or perhaps increase your everyday vocabulary? Where would you like to go? Dream a lot and get in touch with some of your fantasies. What do you want to do to further the kingdom of God on this planet?

Dreams are like the circle of ripples that a pebble thrown into a pond sends out. Rather than constricting the self, dreams expand the self. Do you live your life in such a way—fully, contentedly, and gracefully—that it brings you joy? If not, why not? Dare to dream rather than running away from life.

In the Middle Ages lighting a fire was a tedious process. Once a fire was blazing people would often put a smoldering cinder in a metal box. Little pieces of kindling were then added periodically to keep the spark alive. Then they could start fires easily whenever the need arose.

When we pursue our dreams, we keep our personal spark alive. When others see us lost in the pursuit of our dreams, their dreams begin to emerge.

Regina Carter is a young jazz violinist known for her amazing improvisations. At age 16, Regina was in the audience when the jazz violinist, Stephane Grappelli put on a concert. Regina had studied classical violin since she was four years of age. That night her dream of being a classical violinist was transformed. She said that as she watched this elderly violinist pick up his beloved instrument and start to play, before her eyes his passion turned him into a young agile person. That was the moment when Regina decided to become a jazz violinist.

What is your dream? A dream is an open invitation to become. Participate wholly in your dream. You have nothing to lose. Your value is secure. Agnes De Mille quoted Martha Graham's words in her book, *The Life and Work of Martha Graham.*

> There is a vitality, a life force, an energy, a quickening that is translated through you into action, and because there is only one of you in all of time, this expression is unique. And if you block it, it will never exist through any other medium and it will be lost. The world will not have it. It is not your business to determine how good it is nor how valuable nor how it compares with other expressions. It is your business to keep it yours clearly and directly, to keep the channel open.[68]

Life comes with intricate, interesting work to be done. It is an adventure of imagination. Dreams do become real. We were each created by a loving God in His image. Our God is creative, life-giving. We cannot use up creativity. The more we use it, the more creativity we discover we have.

The more we dream the more we threaten those who have stopped dreaming. Don't be surprised if someone precious to you attempts to keep you from acting on your dreams. Why would anyone do that? Perhaps the person want to keep the relationship the two of you have predictable. Perhaps he or she fears you will outgrow your relationship. Your newfound courage may challenge the comfort level of the relationship. Perhaps they have a dream, but he or she is afraid to step towards it. You must keep moving out in faith obedient to the dream that God has given you.

Dreams bring life and energy. The size of our dreams often illustrates the size of our God. So much in our culture encourages us to shut our dreams down. I've noticed that we as women become particularly obsessed with buying things and feathering our nests when we've snuffed out our dreams. When we don't have a dream so much of our life seems to be about acquiring things or focused on problems. Let's stop sleep-walking through life. Let's dream!

ACTION STEP

In your journal answer these two questions.

If I suddenly found out that I only had one year to live, what dreams would I pursue?

What and who do I allow to stand in the way of living my dreams?

"Dreams are extremely important.
You can't do it unless you imagine it."

GEORGE LUCAS[69]

Move Out of My Comfort Zone

God created us to live in relationship with Him. Our identity is sealed as a result of that relationship. He also created us to live in relationship with people. Our character development and our capacity for intimacy are developed in our relationships with others. God created us to be His image bearers put on earth to influence everyone to whom we relate. We were not created to stay isolated in our comfort zone.

Many women perceive fear, pain, and discomfort as a stop sign never to be questioned or challenged. If instead of pursuing what we want out of life, our highest priority is to avoid being hurt, blamed or held responsible, we imprison ourselves and our self-esteem crumbles.

Jesus Christ has made a radical difference in our lives. Now He calls us to be shining lights in our dark and deceived world. Paul motivates us to action as he writes to the church at Philippi: "so that you may become blameless and pure, children of God without fault in a crooked and depraved generation, in which you shine like stars in the universe, as you hold out the word of life" (Philippians 2:15, 16). In order to shine we need to abandon our comfort zones. If we stay stuck in a comfort zone controlled by fear and a desire to be comfortable at all costs, we are like a mighty lion living in a caged area at the zoo. We may be comfortable, but we are not really experiencing the fullness of life.

Compare the life of the lion in the zoo with the life of the lion roaming in the wilds of Africa. There is no comparison, is there? One lion experiences adventure, while the other experiences apathy.

No one else can ever force us out of our comfort zones. We are the only ones who can choose to move against our fear. As long as we as women push out in our world, as long as we dare to know people and allow ourselves to be known, as long as we speak our truth, as long as we refuse to be content with the status quo, as long as we stretch our capabilities, and as long as we dare to dream, the possibility of failure, of pain, and of rejection increases. That possibility leads to fear and keeps many of us stuck in our comfort zones.

Fear is the little darkroom of life where negatives are developed. Fear is something we permit to paralyze thought. Typically we pull our energy into our center when we are afraid. Therefore we see and hear less at a time that it would benefit us to expand our consciousness. How grateful I am for the Bible and the humanity of its characters. They were well acquainted with fear.

> *Moses*: "I'm not a good speaker."
>
> *Jan's version*: "I stutter, who in the world would even listen to me? I don't want to be humiliated and laughed at."
>
> *Joshua*: "I can't, my family is too poor."
>
> *Jan's version*: " I'm just a kid from the wrong side of the tracks. You wouldn't expect anything of me."
>
> *Jeremiah*: "But I'm too young."
>
> *Jan's version*: "Let someone older do it. I don't have any experience. What will people think? They'll say, Who does she think she is?"

When each of these characters turned their limitations into excuses, God had one response, "I, Jehovah will be with you." Whatever your limitations, Paul's words refute it. "I can do everything through him who gives me strength" (Philippians 4:13).

God's ability is far greater than my anxiety. Faith is the antidote to fear. Feelings can't be controlled. They change just like the weather. Notice them, own them, and do what you need to do in spite of how you feel. Behavior, on the other hand, is controllable.

We fail to move out of our comfort zones because we are waiting for our anxiety to go away. That doesn't work! The only way to be fully alive is to feel the fear, the anxiety, and do it anyway. Be scared to death and do what you have to do.

It's the coward who won't admit that she is frightened. Fear is a God-given emotion when we are moving out of our comfort zone. The good news is fear can be transformed into a companion that accompanies us in all of our adventures rather than being an anchor holding us fixed in one spot.

On the front of a Hallmark graduation card I found a magnificent quote by Eleanor Roosevelt. "You gain strength, courage, and confidence by every experience in which you really stop to look fear in the face. You must do the thing what you think you cannot do."

I also believe that when we stare fear in the face, our faith increases. Bruce Larson wrote these words: "to be saved means to be so secure in God's love—present and future—that I never have to be safe again."[70]

We are not helpless little girls made of sugar and spice; nor are we centerpieces created only to look good; nor are we bitter islands made of stone and ice. We are women who are willing to move out of our comfort zones even when our knees are shaking. Why? Because we have been kneeling on those vibrating knees. Not only do we know who we are, we know *whose* we are. Faith is not the absence of fear. Faith involves facing your fears and moving out in God's power, despite those fears.

Positive Christian women know they accomplish things not because of their fabulous potential, but because they are willing to be vessels used by the Lord. They are willing to risk failure and criticism. They are also aware that failure and success are only temporary.

I had to face my personal fear of failure when the Lord first gave me the dream to put my thoughts on self-esteem into book form. Would you believe I fought the dream for six months? I finally asked myself, "What is the worst thing that could happen to me if I failed at writing this book?" When I put the cold hard realities down on paper, I decided I could live through possible failure far better than I could live with not carrying out my dream because of the fear of failure. Risking is terrifying, yet the option to shrivel up and die is far worse.

To laugh is to risk appearing the fool.
To weep is to risk appearing sentimental.
To reach out to another is to risk involvement.

To expose feelings is to risk exposing your true self.

To place your ideas, your dreams before the crowd is to risk their loss.

To love is to risk not being loved in return.

To live is to risk dying.

To hope is to risk despair.

To try is to risk failure.

But risks must be taken, because the greatest hazard in life is to risk nothing.

The person who risks nothing, does nothing, has nothing and is nothing.

He may avoid suffering and sorrow.

But simply cannot learn, feel, change, grow, love and live.

Chained by his certitudes, he is a slave.

He has forfeited freedom.

Only a person who risks is free!

(ANONYMOUS)

How we need to understand that not trying is the only failure in life. The only way to keep from making mistakes is to do nothing and that's the biggest mistake of all. We are willing to risk because we are not trying to prove ourselves. Our significance and value has been declared, apart from what we do, by Jesus Christ. That allows us to formulate God's dreams for our world and to act on those dreams, until with the Holy Spirit's assistance, they become reality.

God delights in using human beings with their limitations and inadequacies who are willing to be used. He used Mary, an obscure young girl, to be the mother of His only begotten Son. It becomes evident why Mary was chosen when we read her response to Gabriel: "'I am the Lord's servant,' Mary answered. 'May it be to me as you have said'" (Luke 1:38). She could have argued with the angel and let her negative self-concept be an excuse for not allowing herself to be used. It must have been something to hear an angel say to her, "Greetings, you who are highly favored! The Lord is with you" (Luke 1:28). I am so glad that Mary received the affirmation and didn't fight it. I'm glad she believed that with God nothing was impossible. I'm glad she was willing to risk. The question to ask yourself now is this: Am I willing to move out of my comfort zone?

Our commitment as Christian women must be to truth, courage, and honor, not to sameness, security, safety, and staying in our comfort zone. Only then will we feel alive and authentic.

ACTION STEP

Answer this question in your journal.

What would I attempt to do and who would I attempt to influence if fear were not holding me back?

I have found it personally helpful to choose five people (living or dead) as my mentors. These are people who dared to be extraordinary in one way or another. When I am struggling with fear, I often imagine what these adventurers might say to me. Then I write those statements in my journal. I find them a great source of encouragement. Write down the names of the five people you would choose to be the voice of challenge and encouragement in your life. What do you respect about these people? What might they say about a fear you are confronting right now?

"Courage is fear that has said its prayers."

RUTH FISHEL[71]

STEP #27

Live by Priority, Not Pressure

Have you ever felt as if your days were nothing more than a blur of non-stop activity? We pay bills while we're waiting for a doctor's appointment, make phone calls during a little league game, and try to keep up our correspondence while we're stalled in traffic. Often we find ourselves bouncing from one activity to another as if we are a pinball machine. We find ourselves breathless from chasing after the urgent. Most of us don't enjoy the moment because we are rarely in it. Our minds are pre-occupied with what we need to do next or what we haven't gotten to yet. Like Winnie the Pooh we go through life with a dark cloud brewing overhead.

Have you discovered that the scream of the urgent is not the same as the whisper of the important? Julie Morgenstern, a time management expert, who has written an outstanding book, *Time Management From the Inside Out*, suggests that each of us needs to organize our time as we would our closet. Every life is a container with a definite capacity. Each of us has the same amount of limited time.

ACTION STEP

What are the top five priorities that govern your life? List them below. Assign a different color to each priority.

Priority 1:
Priority 2:

Priority 3:
Priority 4:
Priority 5:

Now that you have listed your priorities, go back and check last week's calendar. Did your activities fall under these priorities? Were you a priority? Time for yourself is not only a luxury. It is a necessity. Remember we are operating on full rather than on empty. Adding an oasis to a packed schedule gives us something to anticipate and it helps us get more done in a short amount of time. We don't feel deprived, and as a result we attack what has to be done with more enthusiasm.

If you're like I am, you will discover that unless you consistently check up on yourself, your week will consist of many good but rather unimportant activities if judged against your priority system.

Why don't you chart out an imaginary week, making sure that all entries fall under one of your five priorities? Color each activity according to the priority it fits under. Use a planner and put your to-do's into the actual hour and day you have set aside for that activity. Schedule everything—appointments, calls, errands, bill paying, laundry—on your calendar. Next to the activity calculate both how long it will take you and exactly when you will do it. Record this on your planner. When people ask you if you can do something, you can take the "pause that refreshes" and check your schedule. It will become obvious whether the new option will be a welcome addition to your calendar of not.

When we live our life without priorities, we find ourselves a victim of everyone else's priorities. Letting someone else determine our life script is foolish, dangerous, and irresponsible. At that point we are not good stewards of our time, our abilities or our choices.

Let me stress, once again, that we are God's representatives on planet Earth. We have been designed and appointed to live to the glory and praise of God. None of us want to simply fill up empty space with lots of good but misdirected activities. This automatically happens, I'm afraid, if we don't prioritize. Whatever we choose for our priorities eventually sets the framework for what we will become.

Does it seem overwhelming to start? Often it does, but if you dare to begin, you're miles ahead of many. "And who knows but that you have come to royal position (this place in your life) for such a time as this?" (Esther 4:14).

ACTION STEP

Using a blank weekly calendar list all of your activities including your "to do" items. Color each entry as to the priority it falls under. Make certain that you are a priority on that calendar. Try living from your calendar for two weeks.

In your journal, note how your life has changed for the better as a result of taking control of your calendar.

"Live life, then with a due sense of responsibility, not as [women] who do not know the meaning and purpose of life, but as those who do."

EPHESIANS 5:15 (PH)

STEP #28

Make Goals, Not Excuses

Broadcast journalist Diane Sawyer graduated from college without a clue as to what it was she wanted to do. After she had moved home, her father asked her three questions that would forever change her life. His questions:

"What is it that you love?"

"Where is the most adventurous place you could do it?"

"Are you certain it will serve other people?"[72]

People fall into one of three categories. Either we are dreamers, dream makers, or dream breakers. Diane Sawyer's father was a dream maker. When you review your life up to this point in time, into which category do you fit?

If God were to give you a traffic ticket right now as a result of how you are living your life, what would it be?

A speeding ticket because you are racing through life.

A failure to yield ticket because in relationships it's your way or the highway.

A blocking traffic ticket because you are in the way of other's hopes and dreams.

An illegal U-turn ticket because you've been living in the past.

A driving the wrong way on a one-way street ticket because you need to turn your life around?

(Footnote: When I was going through my files, I found this very clever piece. I have no idea where it came from so please forgive me for not giving credit where credit is due.)

God designed and created us for an extraordinary mission. Our culture and many of its spokespeople influence us towards mediocrity. Dreams, goals, and persistence are not needed for going downhill, but definitely needed for going uphill.

A goal is a dream. It is a game of possibility. It requires a vision, faith, creativity, and willpower. As children of God we must not only set realistic, easily achievable goals, we also need to shoot for the moon. If we miss, we'll still be high. The vision—the dream—will not be compromised. Just pursuing a dream keeps possibility alive. Only accepting perfection does not.

Stravinsky, the composer, apparently once turned down a bassoon player because he was too good to render the perilous opening to the "The Rite of Spring." This heart stopping moment, conveying the first crack in the cold grip of the Russian winter, can only be truly represented if the player has to strain every fiber of his technical resources to accomplish it. A bassoon player for whom it was easy would miss the expressive point. And when told by a violinist that a difficult passage in the violin concerto was virtually unplayable, Stravinsky is supposed to have said, "I don't want the sound of someone playing this passage, I want the sound of someone trying to play it."[73]

An interesting exercise for each of us is periodically to keep a record of all the excuses we make in a given week for not risking something new or for not achieving some goal. I've discovered through keeping a record of my excuses that my attitude is really what holds me back from being all God and I want me to be. It's yet another illustration of an important truth: What happens *in* us is far more important than what happens *to* us.

One day after reading over all my excuses for not accomplishing things, I grouped my excuses under the topics of negative attitude, procrastination, pettiness, inflexibility, self-pity, worry, laziness, lack of discipline, bad habits, and denial. I then went to Scripture to see what God had to say about each one. What an eye-opener! It became crystal clear that God did not want me to limit myself in these ways. Here are the excuses I came up with based on my personal experience. Perhaps you have used one or two of these yourself. Are you curious about what Scripture has to say about each of these attitudes?

Attitudes	What God Says
Negative Attitudes	Colossians 3:17; Philippians 4:8
Excuses	Genesis 3:11–13; Exodus 4:10–12
Procrastination	Ephesians 5:16
Pettiness	Colossians 3:13
Inflexibility	1 Samuel 15:23; Proverbs 29:1
Anger	Proverbs 27:4; Proverbs 27:15
Worry	Philippians 4:6, 7
Laziness	Proverbs 24:30–34
Lack of Discipline	Proverbs 25:28; Galatians 5:22–23
Bad Habits	Hebrews 12:1
Denies Mistakes	Proverbs 28:13

It is not God's will that we limit ourselves and get in our own way. Our lifestyle as Christian women must be a matter of choice, not chance. If we are honest, we know that we can do something specific in the next month that could make our life personally, relationally and professionally worse. Are there specific actions we could take to make it better? You'd better believe there are! How does a dream get converted into reality? It is a five-step process.

ACTION STEP

Write out your dream. Look at it. Ask yourself if it is consistent with your personal values, priorities, personality, and strengths.

Convert your dream into specific goals. Perhaps you could begin by writing one goal under each of your priorities. Goals need to be realistic, attainable, time-related and measurable. How would your life be different if you achieved this goal?

Perhaps one of your priorities is to deepen your relationship with the Lord. One of your goals could then be to set aside 30 minutes each day of the week, beginning today. Or perhaps one of your priorities is to keep growing. An attainable, measurable goal for you might be to read one book every two weeks for the next three months.

The Wheel of Choice

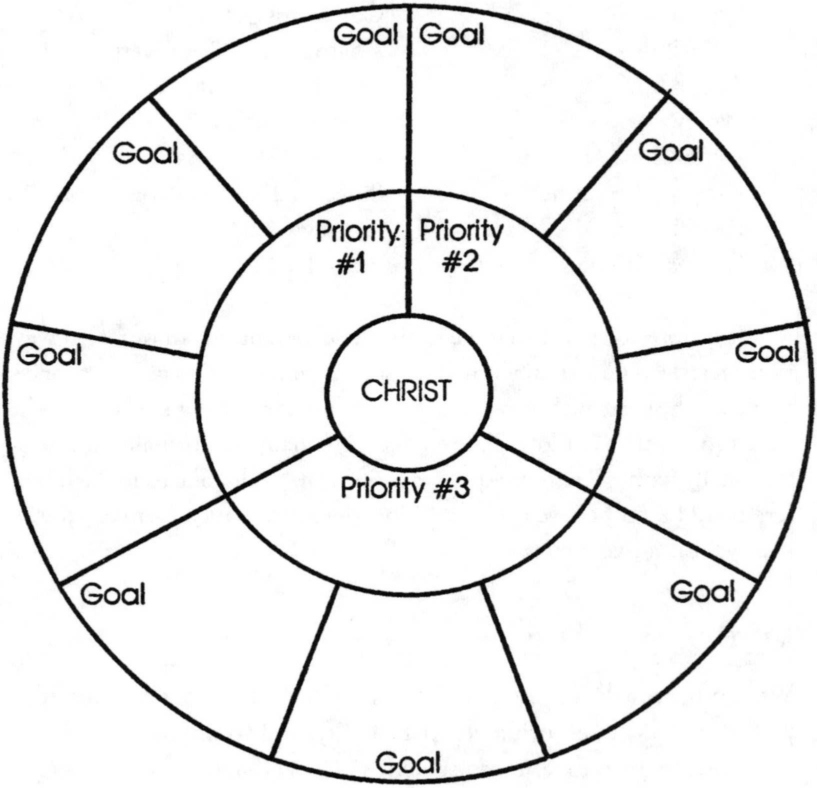

Convert your goal into specific steps.

Steps to Make My Goal a Reality

Goal—a reality

____
(date)

______
#7

______
#6

______
#5

______
#4

______
#3

______
#2

______
#1
Goal—dream

____
(date to begin)

Recruit people to assist you. They might have talents, knowledge and abilities that you lack. They might be people you would delegate tasks to. It's also wise at this step to brainstorm about some of the roadblocks you might encounter. Could these people be valuable in overcoming potential roadblocks? How?

Develop a daily and weekly plan so your goal becomes a realistic part of your lifestyle. Be certain you have broken your goal down into small enough steps so it is attainable. Now record your plan.

Happiness is a by-product of being committed to and involved in something you consider worthwhile. Until we acknowledge some of our own dreams and needs, without sacrificing the needs of those dear to us, we will never fully understand personal fulfillment, which is so essential to healthy self-esteem.

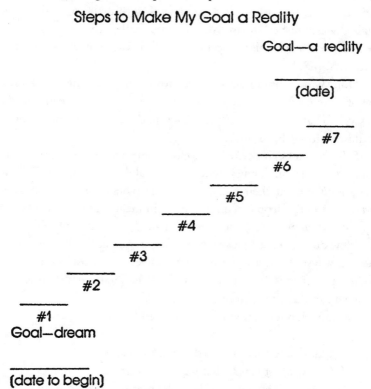

Once you have established you goal, give it all you've got! Your goal is time-dated, but if you don't achieve it within the time frame you originally established, revise your schedule rather than giving up your dream. Most people fail to meet their goals because they never set them in the first place.

Don't worry about your other priorities and goals; just work on the one of primary importance to you. When it becomes a reality in your lifestyle for at least a month, go back and choose another goal you would like to see become reality.

Self-esteem begins with a sense of "I am" that comes from a spiritual center and from being listened to and validated as a child. Once our "I am" is established, then each of us has a deep desire to make a difference and to impact the people in our sphere of influence. Dreams that become goals and then are acted upon result in an "I can" sense of self.

How do you want to leave your mark on planet Earth in small ways and big ways? What are the life experiences you most want to have? What are your most important values? You can make daily choices that move you in the direction of your dreams.

Nelson Mandela dared to dream when he spoke these words:

> Our deepest fear is not that we are inadequate,
> Our deepest fear is that we are powerful … .'
> It is our light, not our darkness that most frightens us.
> We ask ourselves, who am I to be brilliant, gorgeous, talented and fabulous—
> Actually, who are you not to be?
>
> You are a child of God.
> Your playing small doesn't serve the world.
> There is nothing enlightened about shrinking so that other people
> Won't feel insecure around you.
> We were born to make manifest the glory of God within us.
> It is not just in some of us: it is in everyone,
> And as we let our own light shine, we unconsciously
> Give other people permission to do the same.[74]

STEP #29

Know When to Say "Yes!"

One day Moses was standing in the middle of his comfort zone tending the flocks owned by his father-in–law, Jethro, on the far side of the desert. Suddenly his attention was diverted to a bush that seemed to be on fire, yet not consumed by the fire. Moses' curiosity got the best of him. He went over to the bush.

With that action, Moses' comfort zone became permanently shattered. God called to Moses from within the bush, and God let Moses know that He grieved for the misery of His people held bondage in Egypt. Their cries had reached the Almighty God. Now this same God was sending Moses to lead the Israelites out of Egypt. God called a person whose companions for the last 40 years had been sheep, and he wanted this person to provide leadership to an abused, wounded, imprisoned people; a man who had run away in guilt and shame was called to go back to the place of his greatest failure and face his Egyptian "brother" who is now the Pharaoh; a man who had lived in "comfortable" exile was called to face his greatest fear.

God assures Moses of His constant presence. "I AM" both sent Moses and accompanied Moses. Moses asked a question I would have asked: "What if they don't believe me or listen to me? After all, Lord, I certainly don't have a lot of credibility."

At that point the Lord asked Moses a crucial question: "What is that in your hand?" In Moses' case, it was a rod. God asked Moses to offer God that which was in his hand. God would transform it and create miracles with it.

God asks you and me the same question, "What is in your hand?" God wants you to offer that to Him, so that He can use whatever is in your hand to perform His work on planet Earth. Like Moses, will you say "Yes, Lord, use me."

There is a time to say "Yes!"

One Sunday morning I was sick in bed. I turned on the *Hour of Power* and heard Dr. Robert Schuller talking about how we know that it's time for us to say "Yes!" As the Lord so often does, He used those words to set me free to say "Yes!"

The time to say "Yes!" is:

IF the idea comes from God. It would be impossible without Him and the idea in no way contradicts His Word.

WHEN God has made you passionate about the idea and doors open that you can't explain.

AFTER you have committed to God's will. You have counted the cost including the cost of walking away and not pursuing your idea.

WITH at least one support person and, even better, an inner strength group. Surround yourself with people who are gifted in areas that you are lacking.

BUT keep your priorities straight.

BEFORE you know all the answers. Before you know whether it will succeed or be another learning experience. Before you have the whole picture.

As interdependent women, we are called to move out of our comfort zones and impact our world for Jesus' sake. What would you do if you knew you couldn't fail?

ACTION STEP

Write in your journal your response to these questions.

What is your dream?

What is it you would do if you knew you couldn't fail?

Is it time for you to say, "Yes!"?

"Don't wait for something big to occur.
Start where you are, with what you have,
And that will always lead you into
Something greater."

MARY MANIN MORRISSEY[75]

STEP #30

Move Out in Freedom and Gratitude

I believe that every emotionally healthy person shares one attitude in common—gratitude.

In the Gospel of Luke, Luke writes about the ten lepers who called out to Jesus as He traveled along the border between Samaria and Galilee. They pleaded with Him to have mercy on their condition. In response Jesus tells them to show themselves to the priests. As they moved out in faith and started on their journey, they were healed.

When I first read this story, I assumed that all ten of the men would return to express their gratitude to Jesus. After all, their lives and bodies were transformed that day. I was completely wrong. Only one man, a Samaritan, returned to say, "Thank you" and to give glory to God. Jesus' words to the grateful man were, "Rise and go; your faith has made you well" (Luke 17:19). The attitude of gratitude leaves each of us healthy and whole.

God has adopted me into His family. My name has become His name. He is my Provider, Teacher, Savior, Protector, Healer, Defender, Encourager, Restorer, Deliverer, Redeemer, and Affirmer. Do I live with a spirit of gratitude? Do I regularly thank God for the gift of His Son Jesus, for the gift of forgiveness, the gift of unconditional love, of faith, of new beginnings, of opportunities, and of relationship—to mention just a few?

Do I recognize my life and the people in it as treasures from God's hands. If an attitude of gratitude describes me, I don't stand around waiting for the approval of others. I use my energy to affirm the good that I see in others and to tell them what I see. I am no longer competing with others or feeling threatened by their "greatness." You see, I'm free to see and affirm the growth in myself too. My affirmations are focused not just on what they do, but also on who they are. I acknowledge that they make money, but that their money doesn't make them. I affirm their beauty both internally and externally. In small practical ways I attempt to increase others' value.

There is always something only you can do. If you are married your husband only has one wife—you. You have neighbors, children, business acquaintances, or relatives. If you are single, you have a circle of friends unique to you. What one thing can you do in each of these people's lives to raise their self-dignity?

That's your assignment for the rest of your life. You will discover that loving the Father is done by loving those dear people in your life. You will discover what it means to be a woman, an interdependent woman, whose self-esteem comes as a result of being loved by God. A woman whose self-concept is enhanced by loving and speaking encouraging, affirming words to the precious ones God has given you.

For the first time in many of your lives you will understand what it means to be free as a woman. You are:

> Free to affirm your value, but not free to base your value on your performance;
>
> Free to develop your gifts, but not to neglect their use in bettering your world;
>
> Free to pursue excellence, but not to prove your worth;
>
> Free to soar like an eagle, but not to be puffed up with ego;
>
> Free to define who you are, but not to define who I am;
>
> Free to reach out to others, but not to make yourself responsible for their choices;
>
> Free to love, but not to lean;
>
> Free to wear labels, but not be defined by those labels;
>
> Free to be single, but not free to be an island;
>
> Free to be married, but not to forget you are a person;
>
> Free to be a homemaker, but not because there are no other options;

Free to establish a career, but not to escape to utopia;
Free to lead, but not free to lord it over others;
Free to affirm, but not to manipulate, pretend or blame;
Free to hold a child's hand, but not to imprison his spirit;
Free to submit, but not to be a doormat;
Free to define your own needs and dreams and see them become reality, but not at the expense of those you care for;
Free to accept your femininity, but not to deny, degrade, or imitate someone's masculinity;
Free to realize your equality, but not to use it as an excuse for refusing to serve;
Free to talk, but not at the expense of listening;
Free to believe, but not without asking questions;
Free to ask questions, but not to expect all the answers;
Free to be positive, but not to be a Pollyanna:
Free to laugh, but never at the expense of self or another;
Free to be vulnerable, but not free to force me to be;
Free to be creative, but not to the exclusion of relationships;
Free to be hospitable, but not for the purpose of showing off;
Free to pray, but not free to procrastinate;
Free to be involved, but not to be consumed by busyness;
Free to face issues, but not to lose sight of priorities;
Free to state your beliefs, but not free to harbor anger and bitterness when others' beliefs are different from yours;
Free to face intimidation, but not free to be intimidated;
Free to dream, but not to forget that the dreams come from God;
Free to fail, but not to abandon your dreams because you failed;
Free to be interdependent, but not without first examining and rejecting the options of dependent and independence;
Free to see living as a privilege, not as a problem.

JANET CONGO

For the first time in many of your lives you are free to be yourself. You are free to be your own woman, an interdependent woman. Let's never choose self-imposed bondage again.

ACTION STEP

In your journal begin a list of all the people and things you are grateful for.

Spend some quiet time thanking God for everything and everyone on your list.

Is there a practical action or a well-timed word that each of the people in my sphere of influence need to receive? What is it? When will I give it? Over the next few weeks, let each of these people know how precious he or she is to you and how you value this characteristic.

"So if the Son sets you free,
you will be free indeed."
(JOHN 8:36)

"You are God's way of being creative!
You are a woman confident in
God's love and confident of your value.
To God be the glory!"
JANET CONGO

ENDNOTES

Distortions: Confusing Messages

1 Carla Fine, *Strong Smart and Bod-Empowering Girls for Life* (New York: Harper Collins Publishers, 2001), xi.

2 William M. Kinnaird, *Joy Comes in the Morning* (Waco, Tex.: Word Books), 72.

Distortions: Cultural Influences

3 Lisa Kogan, "Blowing Our Cover," *Oprah* (March 2001), 172.

The God I Never Knew

4 Dick Dickinson, "Because God Loves Me," in *Improving Your Self Image* (Eugene, Ore.: Harvest House Publishers, 1983), 52.

5 Philip Yancey, *The Jesus I Never Knew* (Grand Rapids, Mich.: Zondervan Publishing, 1995), 204–205.

6 Eleanor L. Doan, *431 Quotes by Henrietta C. Mears* (Ventura, Calif.: Regal Books, 1970), 71.

7 Yancey, 267.

Why Does My View of God Make a Difference?

8 Rosamund Stone Zander and Benjamin Zander, *The Art of Possibility* (Boston: Harvard Business School Press, 2000), 26.

9 Zander, 30.

10 Bruce Larson, *There's a Lot More to Health, Than Not Being Sick* (Waco, Tex.: Word Books, 1981), 53.

11 Allen Klein, ed., *Winning Words* (New York: Portland House, 2002), 364.

Step #1, Nurture My Spirit

12 Allen Klein, ed., *Winning Words* (New York: Portland House, 2002), 405.

Step #2, Develop My Inner Strength Team

13 William M. Kinnaird, *Joy Comes in the Morning* (Waco, Tex.: Word Books), 133.

Step #3, Face My Past

14 Denis Waitley, *Seeds of Greatness* (Old Tappan, N.J.: Fleming H. Revell, 1983), 44.

Step #5, Let God Heal My Past

15 "The O Interview: Oprah Talks to 4 Phenomenal Women." *Oprah* (March 2001), 184.

Step #6, Celebrate My Uniqueness

16 Marlo Thomas, *The Right Words at the Right Time (*New York: Simon and Schuster, Inc., 2002), xiv.

17 Quotable Quotes, *Reader's Digest* (June 2002), 61.

18 Allen Klein, ed., *Winning Words* (New York: Portland House, 2002), 174.

Step #7, Guard My Self-talk

19 Allen Klein, ed., *Winning Words* (New York: Portland House, 2002), 231.

20 Phillip C. McGraw, *Self-Matters* (New York: Simon and Schuster, Inc., 2001), 252.

21 Nido R. Qubein, *Get the Best From Yourself* (Englewood Cliffs, N.J.: Prentice-Hall, Inc., 1983), 19.

Step #8, Identify My Detrimental Beliefs

22 David D. Burns, M.D., *Ten Days to Self-Esteem* (New York: William Morrow, 1993), 297.

23 Allen Klein, ed., *Winning Words* (New York: Portland House, 2002), 165.

Step #9, Reframe My Story

24 Jim and Sally Conway, *Women in Mid-Life Crisis* (Wheaton, Ill.: Tyndale

House Publishers, Inc., 1983), 54.

25 Allen Klein, ed., *Winning Words* (New York: Portland House, 2002), 25.

Step #10, Evaluate My Tendencies

26 Beverly Engel, *Loving Him Without Losing You* (New York: John Wiley and Sons, 2000), 84.

Step #12, Examine Submission

27 Elaine Stedman, *A Woman's Worth* (Waco, Tex.: Word Books, 1976), 55.

28 John Sterner, *How to Become Super-Spiritual or Kill Yourself Trying* (Nashville, Tenn.: Abingdon Press, 1982), 44.

29 Patricia Gundry, *Heirs Together* (Grand Rapids, Mich.: Zondervan, 1980), 71.

30 David Augsburger and John Paul, *Beyond Assertiveness* (Waco, Tex.: Word Books, 1980), 111.

31 Phoebe Cranor, *How Am I Supposed to Love Myself?* (Minneapolis, Minn.: Bethany House Publishers, 1979), 92.

32 See for reference Janet and David Congo, *LifeMates: A Lover's Guide for a Lifetime Relationship* (Colorado Springs, Colo.: Cook Communications Ministries, 2001).

33 Janice Grana and Carl Koch, *Images: Women in Transition* (Winona, Minn.: St. Mary's Press, 1976), 22.

34 Allen Klein, ed., *Winning Words* (New York: Portland House, 2002), 278.

Step #15, Speak My Truth

35 Harriet Lerner, Ph.D., *The Dance of Connection* (New York: Harper Collins Publishers, 2001), 239.

36 Lerner, 6.

37 Allen Klein, ed., *Winning Words* (New York: Portland House, 2002), 230.

Step #16, Know How to Say "No"

38 Allen Klein, ed., *Winning Words* (New York: Portland House, 2002), 263.

Step #17, Study My Reactions

39 Allen Klein, ed., *Winning Words* (New York: Portland House, 2002), 13.

Step #18, Master My Anger

40 Allen Klein, ed., *Winning Words* (New York: Portland House, 2002), 11.

41 Klein, 10.

Step #19, Embrace Reality

42 Nathaniel Branden, *The Art of Living Consciously: The Power of Awareness to Transform Everyday Life* (New York: Simon & Schuster, 1997), 67.

43 Branden, 79–80.

44 Allen Klein, ed., *Winning Words* (New York: Portland House, 2002), 244.

Step #20, Promoting Change Positively

45 Allen Klein, ed., *Winning Words* (New York: Portland House, 2002), 21.

Step #21, Accept Responsibility for My Own Happiness

46 Allen Klein, ed., *Winning Words* (New York: Portland House, 2002), 337.

47 Klein, 338.

48 Klein, 339.

49 Klein, 339.

50 Klein, 340.

51 Klein, 341.

52 Klein, 346.

53 Klein, 341.

54 Klein, 341.

55 Klein, 341.

56 Klein, 344.

Step 22, Find My Inner Playmate

57 Allen Klein, ed., *Winning Words* (New York: Portland House, 2002), 351.

58 Mark Epstein, M.D., "Play's the Thing," *Oprah* (May 2002), 92.

59 Tim Hansel, *You Gotta Keep Dancin'* (Elgin, Ill.: David C. Cook, 1985), 76.

60 Hansel, 83.

Step #23, Choose to See Possibilities

61 Rosamund Stone Zander and Benjamin Zander, *The Art of Possibility* (Boston: Harvard Business School Press, 2000), 164.

62 Zander, 164.

63 Allen Klein, ed., *Winning Words* (New York: Portland House, 2002), 221.

Step #24, Serve Out of Love, Not Duty

64 Charles R. Swindoll, *Improving Your Serve* (Waco, Tex.: Word Books, 1982), 17.

65 Dottie Versteeg, *To God With Love* (Hagerstown, Md.: Review and Herald Publishing Association, 1980), XXX.

66 Allen Klein, ed., *Winning Words* (New York: Portland House, 2002), 223.

Step #25, Stimulate My Dreams

67 Quoted in Benjamin and Rosamund Zander, *The Art of Possibility* (Boston: Harvard Business Press, 2000), 113.

68 Zander, 113.

69 Allen Klein, ed., *Winning Words* (New York: Portland House, 2002), 186.

Step #26, Move Out of My Comfort Zone

70 Bruce Larson, *There's a Lot More to Health, Than Not Being Sick* (Waco, Tex.: Word Books, 1981), 103.

71 Allen Klein, ed., *Winning Words* (New York: Portland House, 2002), 206.

Step #28, Make Goals, Not Excuses

72 Marlo Thomas, *The Right Words at the Right Time (*New York: Simon and Schuster, Inc., 2002), 76.

73 Quoted in Benjamin and Rosamund Zander, *The Art of Possibility* (Boston: Harvard Business Press, 2000), 103.

74 Zander, 178.

Step #29, Know When to Say "Yes"

75 Allen Klein, ed., *Winning Words* (New York: Portland House, 2002), 277.